Real Estate Investing for Beginners

Earn $10K per Month, Retire Quicker and Relax With No Hassle From Tenants

Mike Hartley

Mike Harley

© Copyright 2023 - All rights reserved.

The content of this book may not be reproduced, copied, or transmitted without explicit written permission from the author(s) or publisher. Doing so would constitute a breach of copyright law and could result in serious legal repercussions for any party participating in the illicit reproduction of the material. Furthermore, due to the nature of intellectual rights, it is impossible to duplicate or replace the original work produced by the author(s) or publisher; therefore, the only way to legally gain access to this content is through direct authorization from either party.

The publisher and the author(s) of this book shall not be held accountable in any way for any damages, reparations or financial losses that may arise because of the information contained herein, either directly or indirectly. This includes any potential harm, monetary loss, or other consequences from individuals' usage of said information. It is also understood that these individuals will not be able to use this clause to evade legal responsibility for their wrongdoings related to the content provided in this book. The publisher and author(s) will thus be free from all liabilities associated with the publication and distribution of this book.

Legal Notice:

This book is subject to copyright protection and should only be used for personal use. Furthermore, it should not be shared with any other individual or persons for any purpose other than that for which it was initially intended. It is strictly prohibited to amend, reproduce, distribute, utilize, quote, or paraphrase any part of the content within this publication without prior authorization from the writer or publisher. Any violation of these regulations may result in legal action against those who have breached them.

Disclaimer Notice:

The presented work is strictly informational and should not be interpreted as an offer to buy or sell any form of security, instrument, or investment vehicle. Furthermore, the information contained herein should not be taken as a legal, tax, accounting or investment recommendation given by the author(s) or any affiliated company, employees, or paid contributors. In other words, the information is presented without considering individual preferences for specific investments in terms of risk parameters. It is general information that does not account for a person's lifestyle and financial objectives. It is important to note that no tailored advice will be provided based on the given information.

The authors and their parent company, along with all employees and paid contributors, have agreed to abstain from trading any stock or investment written about for at least two days publication of any new article, book, report, or email. This includes any equity, options, debt, or other instruments related to that security, stock, or company, except for existing orders that pre-existed the submission; all such charges will be disclosed inside the document. The author(s) may have direct or indirect positions in some of the companies mentioned because of holdings in mutual funds, exchange-traded funds, closed-end funds, or other similar vehicles. Such indirect holdings are usually not disclosed as there is no guarantee that the author(s) is aware at any given time of the individual portfolios of any of these funds. Furthermore, certain decisions by these funds, such as buying or selling stocks, could potentially impact an author's position even if it was not done directly by them.

Warning:

There is no simple, easy way to become wealthy, especially regarding investments in the financial markets. While it may be possible to make a significant return on your investment, there is also a high risk of losing a large amount of money if you do not have the proper knowledge and knowledge base. You must conduct thorough research and analysis to succeed with investments with the most significant potential for price appreciation. Investing wisely requires an extensive level of education and an understanding of how markets work for one's portfolio to yield positive returns over time. Before venturing into any investment endeavor, it is essential to consult an experienced financial advisor or professional who can advise what steps should be taken and how much capital should be invested. It is also necessary to review all relevant information about potential investments, such as the company's financial statements and prospectus, to make an informed decision regarding whether to invest. Everyone must remember that past results are not necessarily indicative of future performance, so it is wise never to invest more money than you can afford to lose.

This work is based upon a thorough analysis of SEC filings, current news events, interviews, corporate press releases, and knowledge obtained through our experience as financial traders, investors, journalists, and educators. We encourage readers to be careful when making decisions involving their finances, as they are ultimately responsible for the outcomes of their choices. To ensure they have thoroughly informed themselves before making any investment decisions, we strongly advise readers to take the time to research each subject in more detail by seeking out additional sources such as third-party analysts or other reading materials on the web. Furthermore, we recommend conducting a comprehensive review of all available data to ensure each conclusion is well-rounded and sound by exploring multiple aspects of an issue or topic. Ultimately, we believe that a person's financial future will benefit from making prudent and informed decisions based on knowledge gathered from various sources.

The author(s) and any parent companies may be affiliated with certain investments offered. If any of these affiliate offers are made, it will be clearly stated, however, that such affiliation exists. It is worth noting that we do not, and would never, affiliate ourselves with companies that do not meet our high standards and ideals; we would not promote anything that we wouldn't consider ourselves, and in that vein, we aim to keep any affiliations with companies that we believe to be of considerable value to our readers, subscribers, and fans. We value your time and education and try our utmost only to offer the highest quality support.

All trademarks, whether registered or pending, are the property of their respective owners.

Foreword to the Series

Investing is a necessary and invaluable life skill that many people don't even realize they need. It allows you to create financial stability, accomplish your most ambitious goals, and secure your future. Whether it be providing for loved ones, avoiding the need to work past retirement age, or funding a dream vacation in Japan, investing requires a deep understanding of the principles of finance as well as those of self-discipline, patience, and sound judgement, free from any emotion or prejudice. While this may feel intimidating at first glance, investing can be extremely manageable with the right guidance and strategies that minimize risks while maximizing returns. By staying informed and educated on the basics of investing, we'll have you on the road to financial success.

Whilst this series masquerades as a comprehensive set of educational guides to the various inroads of investing, it is in fact a chronology of what I have learnt over the years - and from almost every aspect of investing there is. Growing up in a family that had relatively few financial resources, I was always driven to make something of myself and ensure the future security of my loved ones. One of the ways I set out to do this was by ambitiously aiming to make a million dollars in cold hard cash - which seems almost comical when I look back on it now as I had no idea why I chose this figure! A million dollars was just an arbitrary number that I decided upon when I didn't fully comprehend what it meant, or how life-changing it could be. I just thought to myself "I think having a sum of money would really help my family along", so, with this goal in mind, I began researching and investing in various different fields; from stocks to bonds to real estate to swing trading, and so on! My journey has been far from easy, but every step along the way has been incredibly rewarding as I've continued to learn about investing and building my wealth. Now, whilst making money is still a priority/hobby for me, having time with my family is what really matters - and is ultimately more satisfying than reaching any arbitrary figure.

Once I had achieved my goal of amassing a million dollars, it was not that such an amount was not enough; on the contrary, it is certainly a significant sum, and having so much money at once gave me a feeling of great accomplishment. However, I found that I didn't want to stop there. It wasn't just about wanting to make more money; it was about wanting to keep on experiencing the joy and sense of fulfilment from investing. As a youth, I had the dream of being rich and financially free, but with more experience, I now invest because I've learnt to love it! After sixteen years of engaging in this activity, I had finally come up with a system which enabled me to make consistent wins with most forms of investing. So, I figured, why should I let this newfound understanding go to waste? Why should I stop now when things were going so well?

When I decided to start learning about investing, I made sure that I was as prepared and organized as possible. I researched thoroughly, making notes on who offered the best services, the cheapest rates, and which brokerages had a reputation for being trustworthy. As someone who is naturally meticulous, it only made sense to take an in-depth approach to this as well. So, I made sticky notes, wrote in journals, and took copious notes in Word documents - all with the intention of compiling my thoughts throughout the process. Fast forward sixteen years later and here I am writing a series of books based on my experiences!

To ensure accuracy when writing this series from different perspectives - such as in 'Investing for Women' - I asked friends and fellow investors for their input to add further insight into each book. In fact, much of what is written regarding investing has been pre-written by me over time in various forms - be it a scribbled note or a more detailed outline of what I personally needed to know to invest in that field. Although not an expert in all areas of investment, through years of research and experience (and help from others!) I have been able to piece together content that reflects a diverse range of perspectives within this field.

Overall, this series of books is an amalgamation of much of my own research and experiences - some of which I have been continuing the entire time – others of which I've found either not profitable, or only mildly profitable, and so I've ditched them in favour of the better-earning ones! I have also included the thoughts, opinions and input from others involved in the investing world, to ensure accurate representation from a variety of perspectives. It has been a fun journey putting together all the pieces and rewarding at the same time. I am excited to share my knowledge and insight into investing with you all.

This series of handbooks provides a comprehensive guide for even the most beginner investor who is looking to start investing with confidence and ease. Each book dives deep into different aspects of investing, providing readers with the essential knowledge and information they need to make smart decisions when it comes to managing their money. These books are tailored specifically for those who want to gain a better understanding of investing in the financial markets and successfully managing their portfolios over time. Despite my American-based viewpoint, anyone can follow the principles explained within these pages regardless of their country. By reading this series from beginning to end, readers will be equipped with all the key tools necessary for success in investing and achieving long-term financial independence.

In addition to straightforward advice on how to invest, this series also offers guidance on everything from basic stock market terminology to more complex financial instruments. Readers will learn about diversification, risk management strategies, cost/benefit analysis, taxes related to investments, and more – giving them a strong foundation of knowledge that can be applied no matter what type of investment they choose.

My goal is for readers not only to understand what's going on in the markets but also to gain insight into why certain strategies have been useful for me, and how you can find the ones that suit you best.

Note:

I'm often asked what investments I'm presently making and it's an important question for those who are seeking to find financial freedom. After giving the matter a great deal of thought, I felt writing this information down in a book would quickly become outdated since I tend to rebalance my investments at least every three months. To provide readers with more up-to-date information, I decided to create a website which will help them understand what I am doing and encourage them to do the same. This website will not only provides details of the investments but also includes facts and figures that illustrate how these strategies can help people achieve their financial objectives. It will offer guidance on how to make wise investment choices and gives insight into the kinds of risk associated with each decision. Furthermore, this website contains detailed advice on how to maximize returns by diversifying your portfolio across multiple asset classes, mitigating losses through careful analysis of market trends, as well as other long-term strategies for achieving financial independence. By taking advantage of all the knowledge provided on this site, readers can feel confident that they have taken steps towards attaining their own financial freedom.

The journey to uncovering the secrets of successful investing can seem daunting, but I'm determined to make it easier for you! By subscribing to my email list, you'll stay up-to-date with the latest books in the series, and eventually be the first to know about my unique investment system. By being on the e-mail list I will also let you know when the website is launched too – exciting! I am constantly thinking "I wish I'd had this when I started! I'd have saved a decade worth of time!"

So, no matter your level of financial literacy, I have comprehensive information for anyone who is keen on learning more. With an array of resources at my disposal, I can give you an in-depth look at the foundation of successful investing. Through these materials, I will provide a thorough look into elements such as risk management principles and best practices, financial forecasting, budgeting techniques, and so much more.

On top of this knowledge base, subscribers will also be given access to exclusive tools such as calculators and other interactive features that can help simplify complex topics like portfolio construction. This way, no matter what your individual goals are when it comes to building wealth through investments - I'm here to help!

By joining my email list you'll have access to all these resources and more. So come on board for this exciting adventure and discover how you can get started investing for success today!

So, with no further ado, let's dive in!

Your Free Bonus Gifts

Accelerate Your **Learning**

Maximize Your **Earning**

We are here to help you crush it – no bones about it. To make the most of this book, there are two things you'll need:

1. **FREE RESOURCES**

    We have created a number of free resources for you to take advantage of. Use them to accelerate your learning and maximize your earning!

2. **FURTHER RESOURCES**

    We are constantly striving to continue supporting both our team and our students. We are busy creating a website to better highlight all of our investing tips, tricks and current holdings to help our users better see what we're actually up to! To find out when we launch this, and be alerted when we release other titles, just subscribe to our e-mail list and you'll be the first to know!

> THE DAY YOU PLANT THE SEED IS NOT THE DAY YOU EAT THE FRUIT
>
> — FABIENNE FREDRICKSON

"This is my investing mantra. I remind myself daily." — Mike Hartley

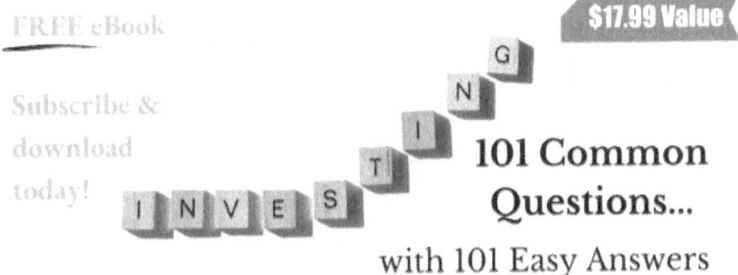

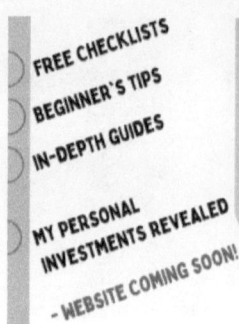

Subscribe To The Newsletter and Join Us!

- Find out the secrets to investing safely
- Join the growing **FIRE** (**F**inancially **I**ndependent **R**etire **E**arly) Movement!
- Live your passive income lifestyle…

www.thefirefund.com/free-gift

Table of Contents

Foreword to the Series _____ vii

Your Free Bonus Gifts _____ xiii

Introduction _____ 5

Chapter 1: The Basics of Real Estate Investing _____ 7

    The Benefits of Investing in Real Estate _____ 7

    How to Get Started _____ 11

    Creating Your Investing Plan _____ 14

Chapter 2: The Different Investing Areas _____ 24

    Residential Real Estate _____ 26

    Commercial Real Estate _____ 30

    REITs _____ 32

    Crowdfunding Platforms _____ 33

    Raw Land _____ 34

Chapter 3: Choose Your Options _____ 36

    Direct Investing _____ 36

    Indirect Investing _____ 40

    Understanding Liquidity _____ 42

Chapter 4: Build Your Dream Team _____ 44

Putting Together the Dream Team _____ 44

Chapter 5: Line Up Financing _____ 50

Different Types of Loans _____ 50

Chapter 6: Start Your Journey _____ 55

Identify Your Financial Stage _____ 56

Pick a Target Market _____ 57

Evaluate Big Picture Location Criteria _____ 59

Evaluate Small Scale Location Criteria _____ 62

Chapter 7: Marketing and Expansion _____ 67

Free and Low-Cost Options _____ 67

Intermediate and High-Cost Options _____ 70

Chapter 8: Analyzing Property _____ 76

Things to Be Considered When Analyzing _____ 77

Chapter 9: Maintenance of Property _____ 87

Using Preventative Property Maintenance _____ 87

Insurance of Your Property _____ 90

Adding Value to Your Property (Renovation) _____ 91

Inspections _____ 97

Chapter 10: Your Real Estate Portfolio _____ 101

Single-Family Business Investing _____ 101

Multifamily Investing _____ 103

Commercial Real Estate Investing _____ 104

Chapter 11: Tax Benefits _____ 108

Real Estate Tax Benefits _____ 108

Conclusion _____ 117

References _____ 120

Mike Harley

Introduction

Property is the next gold mine! You might hear people saying things like this, but the truth is that the property has always been here. It is not some new investment that is taking the world by storm. It is an investment that has been proven to be wealth building over the years. Most of the richest people in the world can attribute at least a good portion of their wealth to property. You can be one of these people too!

You might be looking to get into property investing but have no idea where to start. Let me tell you, this is where a lot of people find themselves. There is all this generic advice about getting into property, but nobody seems to be giving a guiding hand on how exactly to do that. This can be frustrating, but you have come to the right place. I have been in your exact same position. I have tried my hand at investing and, after much trial and error, found success. There are definitely steps that can be taken to lead you to success. I want to help you along the journey.

You probably have some sort of dream or goal in mind. This is a great place to start because it can be your direction. You can reach your property goals when you have the right advice to guide you. There are so many benefits that come with real estate investing. You will be quite surprised, but it is the reason so many people are getting rich doing it and why wealthy people advise everyone to get into it. Property is the gateway to financial security, and it allows you to be in full control. There are many different types of investment vehicles out there, but real estate is unique in what it offers.

Regardless of whether you have some money to burn or only have a few dollars to your name, you need a starting point. This book aims to give you that and then guide you from there. Not everyone's starting point is going to be the same, and that is normal. However, before you are able to make some real estate investments, you will need to understand a bit more about them. You will need a foundation of knowledge that you can build upon. This will help you make well informed decisions as you move forward. That is what the first chapter is going to cover. You will first need to get a grasp on all the basics and then start getting into more detail about how you can invest.

Think of this as your first step towards your goal of becoming a real estate investor. Each time you make a point of taking action, it is going to be another step. I challenge you to think about one actionable thing you can do at the end of each chapter. This doesn't have to be anything big just yet. You just need to be willing to make a move. Many people read books and never apply what they learn. That is not what I want for you. Make a commitment to write down your action step at the end of each chapter and hold yourself accountable to that. You will see that you get a lot more out of this book than you thought possible. Let's dive into the first chapter.

Chapter 1

The Basics of Real Estate Investing

It is a comfortable feeling to know that you stand on your own ground. Land is about the only thing that can't fly away.

–Anthony Trollope

Real estate investing can sound like an amazing idea, but what exactly is it? I think many people have an idea of what real estate investing is but do not know what it entails or how to even start. The beginning of anything can always seem daunting because you simply do not have all the information needed. This is why we are going to take some time and go through the basics of real estate investing. This chapter is going to help set your mindset in the right direction so we can build upon that and ensure you have the right knowledge to continue on your investment journey.

The Benefits of Investing in Real Estate

In order to put real estate in a good light, let's first talk about all the benefits that come from real estate investing. These would be the reasons that many people have decided to start on their investing journey and possibly something you have thought about as well. The thing about real estate investing is that there are so many benefits to it that many people don't even realize it. Fully understanding the scope of the positive aspects of real estate investing can help you make a better decision about it for yourself.

It Brings in a Steady Income

This one is a no-brainer! Real estate investing can bring in a very steady stream of income for you. In fact, the majority of people who decide to invest in property do so because they want additional revenue. Not only that, if you have the correct strategy in place, real estate can be a passive source of income. Passive income is income that you receive without actively making any effort. Most forms of investing will count as passive income because after you have made the initial investment and set everything up, you just have to wait for the money to roll in. There are other types of real estate investing that are not strictly passive but still require less work than a nine-to-five.

Depending on the type of property you decide to purchase, you can end up making a large income that can cover the expenses of the property as well as give you a little extra profit on the side. It is important to do your research on the location in which you want to buy. This will give you the best chance of making the most money, as people will constantly be looking for rentals in that area. We will get into more of the nitty-gritty of property investment in later chapters. For now, you just need to know that you can make a steady income from investing in property.

Financial Security

Financial security is something that many people strive for. When you have a steady flow of income, you will definitely have this type of security. Not only do property investors make money through renting out their properties but also through the appreciation rate of property in general. Over time, property increases in value. This means that a property investor could spend $100,000 on a property and do nothing with it. Then, in 10 years, he could sell his property for a profit. If you own your own property or know somebody who has purchased a property, you know that what they paid for it initially is not the same as the amount they are going to get for it when they sell it. With that being said, there is definitely no guarantee that the value of the property will increase. You need to ensure that you are doing your research so you can pick a property that has growth potential and will ultimately bring in the most profit in multiple ways.

Leverage

Leverage is when you utilize debt in order to make bigger investments. This may sound very confusing but let me give you an example. Let's say you wanted to invest in the stock market. In order to do so, you will need the exact amount of money to purchase the stocks. Let's say you have $20,000 to invest in the stock market. You can purchase $20,000 worth of stocks. You can then wait for your investment to grow and give you a return on it. On the other hand, you could leverage real estate with that same $20,000 and get a much bigger investment. In terms of real estate, $20,000 can get you a $200,000 property. This is because you have a 10% down payment for the property and can take out a loan for the rest of the amount. If you rent out this property, you don't have to pay the $180,000 you actually owe on the property. Instead, you can charge your tenants rent and use their money to pay off the home loan. In this way, you have leveraged $20,000 to purchase a $200,000 asset. The return on investment will not be on the $20,000 you initially had but on the entire $200,000 asset.

Tax Benefits

Most of us can agree on the fact that the taxman puts us under a lot of stress. Nobody really likes paying tax, and if there are ways to get tax benefits, most people will jump at the chance. When you invest in real estate, you can access several tax benefits you wouldn't ordinarily have.

> When you invest in real estate, you are able to deduct 1/27th of the property value from your taxes. You will also be able to deduct the interest you're paying on the home loan.

If you decide you want to be a full-time real estate professional and are classified as such, you can get some huge tax benefits as well. You will need to spend 750 hours a year on your real estate business in order to receive these tax exemptions. You will need this professional designation in order to receive exemptions if you receive $150,000 of taxable income or more. This will allow you to be exempt from capital gains tax, and you can swap one of your investment properties for another through a 1031 exchange (Epperhart, 2021).

You Are in Full Control

When it comes to investing, there's only a limited amount of control that you can have. For example, when you invest in the stock market, you just have to hope for the best. The stock market can go up or down at any point in time, and it is very unpredictable. This is not the same when it comes to real estate investing. If you know what you're doing, you can plan ahead and know that you have full control. The real estate market is much more stable than other forms of investing and this is why you have more control with it. Not only that, but there are many different strategies you can use when it comes to real estate investing. You can choose to house flip, rent out your property, or invest in REITs. These are just a few ways in which you can invest in real estate.

Real estate investing is a skill that you can build within yourself. You can learn how to find good deals, restore cheap properties, and create equity within your investments. How much money you will earn through real estate investing is within your control. This is why many people choose to invest in real estate, as it is a less risky and more stable investment.

How to Get Started

Now that you know all of the benefits that come with real estate investing, you might be thinking about how to get started. First off, you need to decide whether real estate investing is actually for you. Look through the benefits that we have just discussed and think about whether or not you believe real estate investing is going to fit your personality and style. Once you are sure real estate investing is actually for you, you can move on to setting up a plan and strategy going forward. It is really important that you know how to get started so you can put yourself in the best possible position for success.

Set Your Goals

Before you even think about creating a strategy for yourself, you need to decide what your goals are when it comes to investing in real estate. Do you want to create a business for yourself, or perhaps this is just a way for you to diversify your current investments? Your goals will define how you move forward and how aggressively you can invest in real estate. Somebody who wants to create passive streams of income and eventually make real estate their fulltime job will need to have a more aggressive investment plan and more money to spend from the get-go. On the other hand, somebody who is looking to supplement their current income or diversify their investment portfolio can invest at a more conservative rate and build up from there.

How Much Do You Have to Invest?

In order to start investing you will need to know how much money you can actually invest. Real estate investing can require a bit more startup capital than other forms of investing. This means you need to start planning for your investment long before you actually make it. The best way to figure out how much money you have to invest is to look at your current budget and spending spreadsheets. You might need to cut down on certain expenses in order to free up money for investing.

Choose Your Investments

There are plenty of ways in which you can invest in real estate. In order to get started, you will need to look at all of your options and decide what will serve you best. In the next chapter, we will be going through the various types of real estate investing. As you are reading through the chapter, think about whether or not each type of investment is going to work for you.

Start Doing Some Research

Once you understand what type of real estate investing you want to do, it's time to start researching. You will need to find locations for the properties in which you want to invest and decide what is going to be the most lucrative investment for you. Even if you already have a type of investing that you are interested in, there are many options within that. You also need to find properties that are going to serve you best and bring you the most profit. This doesn't happen overnight, and you should expect to spend many hours doing thorough research. This is especially true if you are trying to invest in rental properties or do something like house flipping. You will need to pick the right location and ensure that you can turn around the property to bring you a good amount of profit.

Here is what you can research to make sure you are making the right investment:

- The location should cater to your target market.
- Amenities around the property.
- Crime statistics.
- The neighborhood expected appreciation.
- Level of demand in the area.
- Rental yields of other properties in the area.

Creating Your Investing Plan

Now that you know the basic steps to getting started, you need to buckle down and create your investment plan. I'm not going to lie to you; this is definitely not the most exciting part of the process, but it is foundational. Just like a house, you need to first build a strong foundation so everything you build on top of it is secure. The stronger your foundation is, the bigger your investment projects can be.

> Just like a house, you need to first build a strong foundation so everything you build on top of it is secure. The stronger your foundation is, the bigger your investment projects can be.

You will notice that with many building projects, it can seem like nothing is happening when they are building the foundation. If you have a building project in your area, you are likely to drive past it and see nothing for a good few months. Even though there are lots of construction vehicles and people seem to be doing something, you do not see the actual building for a long time. In many cases, you might even think the building site has been abandoned or the workers are incompetent because there is no progress. However, as soon as the foundation is built, the rest of the structure is erected quite quickly.

Over the course of a few weeks, the entire building starts to take shape, and it seems like progress accelerates. This is because building a foundation takes longer, and if you get it wrong, starting from the beginning can be taxing and painful. Most architects and engineers know this. This is why they spend so much time ensuring that the foundation is strong. When it comes to investing, you need to make sure your foundation is strong so that when it comes time to spend your money, you can do it at an accelerated rate and see the benefits quickly. Your investment plan is going to be your foundation.

Set SMART Goals

When looking at the title of this section, you might be thinking "smart" as in clever. However, SMART is an acronym that can actually help us achieve our goals in a much better and more effective way. There are five main principles to goal setting that will help you better reach your goals, no matter what they are. Even though we are going to be talking in the context of real estate investing, you can use this method to set any kind of goal in your life. This is why this method is so valuable and helpful.

Specific

The S stands for specific. One of the biggest mistakes people make when it comes to setting goals is setting them too big or too broad. A specific goal will be something that you can actually achieve because you can set clear-cut parameters within which to operate. It is very difficult to focus your efforts and stay motivated to achieve your goals if they are not specific.

If you struggle to set specific goals, then try asking yourself a few questions. I like to call these the 5W questions. You will be asking yourself, "What?" "Why?" "Who?" "Where?" and "Which?" This will help you to narrow down exactly what your goals are so you can set a plan in motion in order to reach them. Let's look at an example of a vague goal versus a specific goal.

Vague goal: I am going to start real estate investing.

Specific goal: I am going to purchase and rent out a two-bedroom apartment.

The specific goal shows you exactly what you need to do. You know that you will be looking for a two-bedroom apartment and can focus your efforts on this. Simply saying you are going to start real estate investing is way too broad for you to actually take action. This is the problem with vague goals, you simply are unable to take steps to reach them.

Measurable

The M stands for measurable. Every goal you set needs to be measurable in order to track your progress and understand how much further you need to go. Measurable goals are also more motivating because you can see how far you've come and how far you still have to go. You will be able to assess your progress and decide whether you need to change your strategy or not. Think about it. You are far more likely to finish a project if there is a deadline than if you are free to do it whenever you'd like. Deadlines and numbers actually keep us motivated and accountable. We feel excitement as we get closer to achieving our set goals, and this helps us speed forward.

In order to set a measurable goal, you need to know how much, how many, or how you will know if the goal is accomplished. Using the example from the specific goal, let's see how we can change this to also be measurable.

Specific goal: I am going to purchase and rent out a two-bedroom apartment.

Measurable goal: I'm going to purchase a $300,000, two-bedroom apartment. In order to do this, I need to save $60,000 as a down payment.

With this goal, you know exactly how much you need to save for the down payment as well as the total amount the apartment should cost you. You can now make a plan to start saving for this down payment. You have a specific number to work towards, and as you get closer, you will start to feel more motivated.

Achievable

The A stands for achievable. One of the biggest traps people fall into when they set their goal is shooting too high. This doesn't mean that you have to limit yourself or downplay what you're capable of. You just need to be realistic when setting your goals. Your goals actually need to be achievable if you have a chance of getting there. While you might be excited to start your real estate investing journey, setting yourself a goal to purchase five properties in the span of four years isn't really realistic. Most people won't be able to achieve this, and it can lead you to being disheartened and giving up completely.

In the above example when we set a measurable goal, we were able to put numbers to our specific goal. This is great, but the numbers we have set might not be realistic for you. So let's tweak the measurable goal we have set to something more achievable for someone who has a limited budget to start with.

Measurable goal: I'm going to purchase a $300,000, two-bedroom apartment. In order to do this, I need to save $60,000 as a down payment.

Achievable goal: I am going to purchase a $150,000, two-bedroom apartment. In order to do this, I need to save $30,000 as a down payment.

While it might have been amazing to purchase the $300,000 apartment, for somebody who does not have enough to make a good size down payment, it's not going to be an achievable goal. It might take far too long to save the money for the down payment, and the person might struggle to get a mortgage of that size. In this case, setting something that is more achievable is the best option. Since this is just the beginning of the investment journey, a smaller property is still a good choice.

The main goal is to start real estate investing, and when you set an achievable goal, you will be able to get there at a reasonable pace.

> The main goal is to start real estate investing, and when you set an achievable goal, you will be able to get there at a reasonable pace.

Relevant

The R stands for relevant. It is important that every goal you set be specific and relevant to you. It needs to be something that matters to you personally, so you will want to achieve it. This will help you maintain control over all of your goals and ensure that you are doing them for the right reasons. In order for a goal to be relevant, you need to make sure that it is worthwhile and that it is the right time for you to reach it. The end product should be able to match the efforts needed to get there. You also need to make sure you have access to the resources needed in order to reach the goal. These can be hard questions to answer, but it is important to sit down and think about them.

Real estate investing might not be for everyone, depending on their life situation. It is definitely something that every person can work towards, but it's important to be honest about where you are in your life and what is truly important. For example, while real estate investing might be incredibly important to you,

you might have another responsibility that's taking up most of your resources. In this case, you could look into pausing your real estate investment journey until you can take care of your other responsibilities. Once that is done, you can then refocus on real estate investing.

Time-based

The T stands for time based. Every goal you set needs to have

a target date tied to it. This is a deadline that you need to meet. Let's take it all the way back to when we were still in school or university. Every test, project, or exam we had to do came with a deadline. If we did not produce the required work by the deadline, we would fail or not get the desired result or mark we wanted. The deadline was what motivated us to study or do the project. I can guarantee you that most students would never write their exams or submit their projects if there wasn't a deadline. Having a goal that is time-based keeps us motivated and helps us plan better. It is also easier to set a measurable goal if there is a time bound aspect to it. It allows us to break down bigger goals into smaller sections so we can reach them. Let's look back at our achievable goal and see how we can turn it into a time based goal.

Achievable goal: I am going to purchase a $150,000, two-bedroom apartment. In order to do this, I need to save $30,000 as a down payment.

Time-based goal: I am going to save for the $30,000 down payment over the course of three years.

Putting a timeframe on it allows you to see how far you need to go and how long you have to do it. You can then break down your goal into smaller pieces so you can work towards them on a yearly, monthly, or weekly basis. This makes things a lot easier to do. In the above example, where you have three years to save $30,000, you will need to save $10,000 every year. If you were to break this down further, you would need to save just over $800 per month for the next 36 months. This seems a lot more achievable than the $30,000 lump sum you are looking at. You can make adjustments to your budget to free up $800 every month. You might look at taking on a few extra shifts at your job or starting a side hustle in order to increase your income. Perhaps you can cut back on certain luxury items in your budget in order to funnel money into your real estate investment fund. As you can see, creating a SMART goal makes things easier to achieve. You can set step-by-step processes so you know exactly how to get to your goal. When a goal is too vague, it becomes very difficult to set a plan in motion. This is why it is a good idea to take some time to sit down and set a goal that you can achieve and measure your progress against. You will be so thankful that you took the time to do this because it makes your goals so much more tangible.

Be Accountable

Now that you have your goals set in stone, it is important to be accountable to yourself. You are not going to be able to reach your goals unless you are consistent with the effort you're putting in. This is why we broke it down into a monthly basis when we were talking about the previous goal. It is easier to hold yourself accountable every month than to get to the end of the year and realize you haven't done what is needed in order to reach your goal. Creating check-in points for yourself is going to really help you stay accountable. You can check in with yourself every month, every quarter, and every year. You can reassess how far you've come and decide whether or not you need to change your plan.

Create Celebration Checkpoints

When you set a long-term goal, it can be very difficult to stay motivated throughout the process. This is why you should create celebration points for yourself. When you break down your goals, you can create mini-goals. Once you reach these smaller goals, you can give yourself a reward. This gives you something to work toward in the short-term. Every quarter you reach your savings goals towards your real estate investment, you can take yourself out to a nice dinner or buy something you really like. Perhaps you can treat yourself to something you ordinarily wouldn't. This is a small reward that you can work into your lifestyle and that keeps you motivated. This also helps you keep track of your goals so you can make changes when necessary.

Be Willing to Change Strategies

As you start real estate investing, you might realize that what seemed like a good idea is no longer fitting for you. It is actually quite common to start off with a certain plan and, as you do more research, realize that this might not be the best option for you. Perhaps you come across an even better goal or find a strategy that's going to work better for you. There is no shame in pausing and rethinking your current strategy. In fact, it is far better to do this than to force yourself to stick to your original plan only to reach your goal and have it not been what you want it to be.

Investment plans often change over the years. Our goals change and the amount of resources we have might also change. Just because you were only able to save and invest $800 in your 20s doesn't mean that you have to stick with this for the rest of your life. In your 30s or 40s, you might realize that your disposable income increases and you are able to invest more. In this case, you can definitely change your strategy in order to invest more aggressively. Doing a yearly check in with yourself is a great way to ensure that the goals you have stated are still relevant for you. You can take a look at your finances as well as your current stage of life to see what needs to change.

Chapter 2

The Different Investing Areas

Ninety percent of all millionaires become so through owning real estate.

–Andrew Carnegie

When people think of Real Estate investing, they simply think it's purchasing a property. However, as there are many different ways you can invest in real estate. This makes it an incredibly flexible investment, and it can suit even a beginner. It is a good idea to look through all the various types of real estate investing and then decide which one is going to be best for you. Not every type of real estate investment is going to be a wise choice for you specifically. We are going to go through the various types to help you make a decision and fully understand each one.

Let's first discuss what actually makes a good real estate investment. A good investment will be one that has the highest chance of success and a high return on your investment. If there is too much risk involved without any potential reward, then it isn't going to be a good investment. Any kind of risk you take needs to be balanced out by the possibility of a high reward. Even if you were to choose an investment that has a high chance of success, there's definitely no guarantee. All investments carry some sort of risk, but we do them in order to get the potential reward. With this being said, you shouldn't be investing in real estate if you don't have the money to lose. If you are in dire need of extra money, it is a recipe for making bad investment decisions. Your mind is clouded, and you are relying on the investment to help make ends meet. This almost never works.

> Any kind of risk you take needs to be balanced out by the possibility of a high reward. Even if you were to choose an investment that has a high chance of success, there's definitely no guarantee.

With this being said, I'm definitely not suggesting that you should have $1 million in the bank in order to start investing in real estate. Since there is a lot of diversity when it comes to investing, you can still start with a small amount. If you're looking to purchase a property, you only need a certain percentage in order to make a down payment. The rest will be covered by a mortgage loan. In this case, you should have a good-sized down payment before you start thinking about investing in physical properties. Have a look at the various ways you can invest in real estate to see which one suits you best.

With this being said, I'm definitely not suggesting that you should have $1 million in the bank in order to start investing in real estate. Since there is a lot of diversity when it comes to investing, you can still start with a small amount. If you're looking to purchase a property, you only need a certain percentage in order to make a down payment. The rest will be covered by a mortgage loan. In this case, you should have a good-sized down payment before you start thinking about investing in physical properties. Have a look at the various ways you can invest in real estate to see which one suits you best.

Residential Real Estate

When thinking about real estate investing, most people start off by picturing residential real estate. Essentially, you will be a landlord. You'll be owning a property that you can either rent out or flip in order to make money. Basically, you are purchasing a property that other people can live in. The great thing about residential real estate is that you can use it the way you want to. You can opt for short-term or long-term leases depending on how much time and effort you want to put into your property. Residential real estate tends to be less sensitive to the conditions of the economy. This makes it a more stable investment. The truth is, people will always need a place to live, regardless of the state of the economy. Even if you have to change your pricing strategy a bit, you will still be making a good amount of money from your investment.

It is much easier to get financing for residential real estate than it is for commercial or other types of real estate. You can get a 15- to 30-year mortgage, which is available from many different providers. This makes it one of the most affordable ways to invest in real estate, and you only have to pay the down payment as your investment. The rent you receive from your tenants or the amount you get from flipping the house will take care of the rest of the mortgage. If you make a good down payment, it will be easy for a tenant to pay off the rest of the mortgage, so the barrier to entry into this type of real estate investment is not too high.

If you are looking into residential real estate investing, location is key. If you're able to pick the right location, then you can make a massive profit throughout the duration of owning the property. The first thing you need to do is decide what kind of residential real estate investing you are looking into. If you are looking at short-term rentals, like Airbnb, you'll need to pick a location that is close to amenities and tourist attractions. This will allow you to get a steady stream of guests who want to pay to stay in your property. If you are looking for more long-term rentals, you would be looking to purchase somewhere that's going to target the type of people you want to attract. For example, if you are targeting single businessmen, you might look at investing in an apartment that is close to the city. If you are targeting larger families with small children, you would need to invest in a suburb that is close to schools and is quite safe. Think about the needs of your target resident, and then decide on the location they would want to live in. From there, you can look into purchasing the right property. This method will also apply to house flipping, as you would need to purchase the property, flip it, and sell it to someone who wants to buy the property.

House Flipping

Let's take a break here and discuss what house flipping is. I have mentioned it a few times but never truly explained what it is. It is actually a very simple concept. All you need to do is purchase a property for as little as you can. You will then renovate and redecorate the house to make it more valuable and functional.

After that, you will put it back on the market to sell it for more money.

When you are flipping a house, you need to make sure you are purchasing a property that you will be able to sell in a few months or a year. House flipping needs quite a quick turnaround time, as you are not going to be making any money from it until you sell the house. This is why it's a good idea to do your research when you are purchasing a property. You need to pick a property that will sell for less but is not going to require extensive renovations in order to put it back on the market. You will also need to consider how much money the renovations and redesigning of the house will cost. You still want to make a good profit, so make sure you're not spending too much money on renovating the home. It does take a keen eye and some experience to do this effectively.

Long-Term vs Short-Term Rentals

If you decide that house flipping is not for you, long-term and short-term rentals are great ways to make money through real estate investing. The strategy you choose will depend on how much time you have to devote to your rental property and the general financial strategy that's going to work best for you. They both have their benefits as well as their drawbacks, so it is a good idea to take some time to think about it before you make your decision.

Long-term rentals are when you sign a lease for 6 to 12 months or even longer. You will be finding a tenant to live in your property, and they will be paying you rent each month or at stipulated dates. You will have a steady income throughout the duration of the lease, and you don't have to do anything. This is a great way to make passive income because you don't have to do much to the property while there are people living in it. You do have some responsibilities to take care of the property and fix any problems your tenants are facing. However, if the property is well taken care of this shouldn't be too much of a worry. If you are looking into long-term rentals, it is a good idea to research what expectations a landlord has in the specific state you have your property in. There are also some legal obligations that you should be aware of. It is a good idea to have all your bases covered in this regard.

When looking into long-term rentals, you need to make sure you choose your tenants wisely. It can be very difficult to remove a tenant before the lease is up, and it can be quite stressful to do so. If you take some time and verify the people you have living on your property, this is going to go a long way. Make sure you have done all the relevant background checks and are comfortable having the person live on your property. You also need to set out clear expectations and rules that should be in the contract. This way, if there is a breach of contract, you will have grounds to take legal action if necessary.

Short-term rentals are more like vacation rentals. Airbnb is a great example of this. People will be looking to stay at your property for a short time, usually for business or on vacation. The type of people you target will depend on the location of your property as well as the type of property you have. You can make a good amount of profit from short-term rentals, and if you do it right, you definitely can make more than with a long-term rental. People are willing to pay a higher rate per night than they are when they are renting something for the long-term. With this being said, short-term rentals are a lot more work. You have to make sure you have the time to turn around the property for the next guests. You also have to put forth an effort to find new renters consistently. This means you have to spend some money on marketing to ensure your property's name gets out there.

If you do not have the time to cater to your guests who stay in your short-term rental, you can consider hiring somebody to do it for you. This way, you can turn shorter rentals into a more passive form of income. There are costs involved with this, so make sure you are able to charge enough on a nightly rate to cover these costs. We have another book called *Passive Real Estate Investing* which can help if you are interested in making this a passive source of income for yourself. You won't have to stress out about the day to day running of the property, so you can spend time on other things. You also want to ensure that your guests' experience is the best it possibly can be, so this does take some additional effort, and you will have to consider the decor and the amenities. In most cases, the short-term rentals that do best will be the ones that get the best reviews and offer the best guest experience.

Commercial Real Estate

Let's switch gears and talk about commercial real estate. A commercial property is one that's going to be used for business related purposes. This could be perceived as providing a place for people to work rather than for them to live. Commercial real estate is typically leased out to people who want to conduct activities that will generate income. Office buildings and office parks are examples of commercial real estate. It can also include storefronts and shopping centers. There are various forms a commercial property can take. Anything from an office building to a duplex, restaurant, or warehouse will be included under the umbrella. You can make money from commercial real estate by either leasing it out, reselling it, or holding it.

There are some businesses that own the property they occupy, but in most cases, businesses will rent out an office or a building for their business activities. An investor or a group of investors will own a collection of buildings or simply one building and collect rent from each of the businesses that operate within its walls. The commercial lease can run for a very long time. The lease can typically range between 5 and 10 years, but you can also get one that is one year long. There are some commercial real estate investors that do leases on a more short-term basis or on a month-to-month basis. Typically, the length of the lease will correspond to the size of the space being rented out.

If you're looking to just be an investor and don't want to get involved in all of the nitty-gritty of taking care of the property, then employing a real estate management firm is a good option. It is more difficult for beginners to get into, but if you are willing to put in the effort, it can be a very lucrative form of real estate investing. They will handle everything from overseeing the leases to managing and retaining tenants. Since they have specialist knowledge it is usually a good move to make because they fully understand all the rules and regulations that govern a commercial property based on the country and state they are in.

There are two ways in which a real estate investor can make money through commercial real estate. This is a direct or indirect investment. A direct investor will become a landlord by owning the actual property and renting it out to businesses. Investing in commercial property is definitely a high risk or high reward situation. Even though it is not the easiest way to invest in real estate, with the right guidance, it can be done. Choosing the right approach is crucial for this type of real estate investment. This is why research and doing your best to prepare will be your best friends here.

REITs

This is a great option for investors who are looking to add real estate to their portfolio but don't want to get involved in the traditional real estate market. REIT stands for real estate investment trust. A corporation, also known as a trust, will pool together investor money in order to purchase properties to generate an income. A REIT can be sold and bought on all major exchanges. In this way, it functions like any other stock on the market.

An REIT will provide regular income to an investor. This is done through dividends. Any corporation will need to pay out 90% of all taxable profits in order to maintain the status of an REI. This way, the company or corporation will not be liable for corporate income tax. And REITs can help an investor get into residential investments such as office buildings or shopping malls without having to purchase them directly. They are also highly liquid, which is not true of most types of real estate investments. Since you do not own the actual property, if you want to liquidate your investments, all you have to do is sell your REIT as you would a regular stock in the market.

Crowdfunding Platforms

Crowdfunding is a great way to raise money in order to start investing in building a business. There are tons of people who use crowdfunding and have founded successful businesses and investments. A crowdfunding platform allows you to advertise your idea to potential investors and individuals. You can utilize social media outlets and other platforms to reach a specific audience that would be interested in investing in your idea. Many people are able to invest a smaller amount, so you can generate larger sums of money quickly. All investors who have given you money will become shareholders in your real estate property or company.

You can either start a crowdfunding campaign on your own or find one to invest in. If you do want to invest in a crowdfunded real estate campaign, there is typically a minimum amount you will need to invest in order to get started. This can vary depending on multiple criteria. It is a good idea to do your research to find out how much the minimum is. One of the biggest risk factors associated with crowdfunding is that you are putting your money into something that is essentially unknown.

People are trying to get their real estate ventures off the ground, and it is not guaranteed that it will work. This means there is the potential for you to lose all the money you have invested.

Raw Land

Raw land investing is when you choose to invest in a plot of land that has not yet been developed or even prepared for construction. Basically, the land is completely untouched and undeveloped. It is an entirely different ballgame than investing in traditional real estate methods. It does take some knowledge and strategy to do this properly because it can be risky. This is more of a long-term strategy because you would need to do something with the land in order to resell it or generate some kind of income from it. You could invest in the land and continue on to commercial or residential investments, crop and livestock operations, or farmland investing.

Another strategy that raw land investors employ is to purchase the land and wait for it to appreciate in value. Typically, land does appreciate in value throughout the years because we only have a limited amount of it. Since there are investors who are always looking to build new properties for various reasons, people are on the lookout for untouched land. You can purchase raw land for a low price and hold it until the right investor comes along to purchase it from you for a specified price.

If you want to maximize your investments, you will need to do a lot of research on the land you are trying to purchase. You will need to look for land that you can afford but that will also be in demand at some point. There is no point in buying land in a very small area that investors are not looking to purchase in. The goal should be to find inexpensive plots of land that have potential for future growth and building prospects.

If you are able to buy a larger plot of land, you have the option of breaking it down into smaller plots. This way, you have several plots of land that you can sell or develop for different reasons. This can increase the amount of money you make through your land investment. You can also choose to lease the land for a number of reasons and then collect the rent. Many people might be looking for a large plot of land for various reasons, such as events. If you are in a desirable area, you can make a good amount of money from this.

The type of real estate investing you start doing will be highly dependent on how much money you have available as well as your time and interests. Since there is a lot of flexibility when it comes to real estate investing, you are bound to find a specific type that suits your needs. It is important to understand what you're getting into and ensure that you are doing the right research to maximize your returns in the future. Real estate investing can be incredibly exciting, but you do have to go into it with your eyes open. If you do that, you will definitely see success in your real estate investment journey.

Chapter 3

Choose Your Options

Real estate is an imperishable asset, ever increasing in value. It is the most solid security that human ingenuity has devised. It is the basis of all security and about the only indestructible security.

–Russell Sage

The great thing about real estate investing is that there are many options to choose from. You are free to pick the ones that suit you best and work from there. It is always a good idea to understand what is available so you can make the right choices.

Direct Investing

Direct real estate investing is the most traditional form of real estate investing. Chances are that you were thinking about this type of investing when you first decided you wanted to invest in property. Direct investing is when you purchase the property or a portion of it. You will make money by renting it out to other people, selling it at a higher price than you paid for it, or allowing business activities to run through your property and charging a fee for the use of the property.

Pros

There are many positives to investing in direct real estate. We are going to go through these in detail to help you see why direct investing could be for you:

- Firstly, you give yourself the opportunity to really increase your income if you do it right. You will also be able to get tax breaks from this type of investing which can free up even more cash for you to invest or put into other areas of your life. If you work with a tax accountant, you will be able to take full advantage of this.

- Since property already has value that appreciates through the years, it is definitely lower risk than many other types of investments. You do have to ensure that you are picking a property and location that has potential growth but if you have done the initial research, you should be on the right track. If you do purchase a good property, the likelihood of its price increasing in a few years is quite high. This means you don't have to do much in order to make a profit from property. If you want to increase the value even more, then you will need to decorate and spend some money on the presentation before reselling it. You would be surprised at how much value a new coat of paint can add to a property.

- Investing directly in property puts you in the driver's seat. You will have full control over what you do and how you do it. Since there are many ways, you could make money and increase the value of a property, you are free to pick the strategy that suits your needs and capacity best.

- You also have a tangible investment where you can physically pick out the location, types of property, and the financing structure. For those who want to be fully involved in their investments direct investing is the way to go.

These are just a few of the positive aspects that come with direct investing in real estate. You are the one who gets to make all the decisions, and this is one of the few investments where you have something solid and tangible to show for it.

Cons

While there are so many positive aspects to direct investing, in order to make a balanced decision, you also need to know about the cons. Many people don't like to look at the negatives because they believe it will talk them out of making the choice they want to make. However, this is not true. In fact, knowing the potential downsides can actually help you prepare in advance for the future. You are able to go into it with your eyes wide open. You can think of it like a marriage to the person you love. Even though you know there might be some flaws and you fight sometimes, it is definitely not enough to not solidify the commitment. People who only know the good of the other person have unrealistic expectations of them and end up getting hurt and disappointed in the end.

Knowing the potential bad can help you navigate them better, and it also helps you appreciate the good much more.

For all the positives of direct investing, one of the biggest downsides is that it requires a lot of effort. You need to do a lot of research when it comes to buying a property. This can take hours of putting your head down in order to find the right investment opportunity. It is not uncommon for a real estate investor to spend many months, or even years looking for the perfect investment property. Once the property is found, you will now have to put in the work to turn it into a profitable investment. Regardless of whether you are thinking of flipping the property, becoming a landlord, or running an Airbnb, you will need to put in continuous work. The property is yours to maintain and take care of. Any plumbing emergency, electrical fault, or similar situation will need to be sorted out as quickly as possible.

There is also the issue of finances that needs to be considered. Purchasing a property requires a lot of capital. This is definitely one of the most resource intensive investment vehicles. If you don't have the cash upfront, you will need to seek out a loan from the bank or perhaps get other investors on board with your plan. Thinking about the financial side of things is really important because there's always a chance that you don't find tenants quick enough or the market could drop, resulting in you having to pay more out of pocket than expected.

Since real estate is quite illiquid, it will take some time before you are able to turn a profit from your investment. Even if you want to sell to get your money back, it can take several months to find an appropriate buyer. This is why it is very important to fully understand real estate and what it takes to invest in it.

These are the main negative points that come with direct investing in real estate. These things can be navigated if you plan for them in advance. You can ensure you are financially prepared for your investment so that even if things do take more time, you will be able to handle it before you start making a profit. The cons are not meant to deter you but to help you prepare well.

Indirect Investing

When you invest in real estate in an indirect manner, you aren't actually purchasing a physical property. REITs are the most common type of indirect real estate investing, where you purchase shares in a company or fund that invests in real estate. You still benefit from the real estate market, but you do not have to own any physical property.

Pros

People who want to get into real estate investing but do not have the means to purchase a physical property choose the indirect route. This is because it is much easier to get into.

You can choose the indirect route if you need a lower barrier to entry or if you want to dip your toe into the market, for example:

- You do not have to have a large sum of money or take

out a loan in order to start. All you have to do is sign up and get started. The barrier to entry is much lower, and this makes it a great choice for those who are just starting out with real estate investing.

- It is a lot more stable in terms of your yearly return on investment, and some can offer dividends, just as some stocks do.

- Another huge positive is the fact that indirect investing is completely liquid. You could sell up and take your money out almost immediately. You don't have to worry about marketing and selling a property, which could take months. If you need your money for another investment opportunity or you run into an emergency, you have the freedom to take it out and do what you want with it.

Cons

Even though you are investing indirectly in real estate, everything will be responding to the real estate market. It is important to remember this as we discuss the cons of this type of investing (Folger, 2021):

- Interest rates on the market can have a huge negative impact on your investments. You also have to consider the tax side of things. In many cases, an indirect real estate investment is taxed at a higher rate because the dividends are usually classified as "non-qualified dividends."

- You can use an indirect real estate investment opportunity to diversify your current portfolio, but you should be wary of making this your only type of investment. Most of the funds and companies that run indirect investments for individuals do not diversify their actual investment. This means there is a risk of losing all your investment capital should the market take a dive. For example, a REIT could be based on office parks and other business centered properties. If we look at what happened in 2020 with the pandemic, there was less demand for this type of property. People started working from home, and companies canceled their leases on their office spaces. Anyone who had their money invested in this type of REIT would have suffered a loss. There are always property specific risks to take into account when investing this way.

Understanding Liquidity

Liquidity is important to understand when you are investing. Liquidity is all about how quickly or slowly you are able to take your assets, sell them, and make your money back. Some people believe that there is more risk when it comes to assets that are less liquid. However, this is not always the case. Having liquid assets does make things more flexible for the investor but it is definitely not the be all and end all of investing.

If you are investing directly in the real estate market, you are most likely taking on illiquid investments. This is because it will take some time to sell and get your money out of the investment. Your money will be tied up for an extended period of time. This is why you should never have all your money in direct real estate. If an emergency were to pop up, you would have no way of dealing with it. Having some investments that are liquid is really important to your financial health.

> Having some investments that are liquid is really important to your financial health.

Before you think that investing in direct real estate is a bad thing because of the liquidity factor, there are some definite benefits to it. Long-term investments often do better when they are not liquid. This is because it gives the market more time to work for you. When you are investing in real estate, it will be a long-term thing in most cases. Having this in mind means that you can take advantage of an illiquid investment. When it does come time to cash out, you will have made a huge profit. Not only that, but if you choose to rent out space on your property, it could be a source of income for the foreseeable future, and you never have to sell. There are not many other investments that give you the security and benefits of real estate in this sense.

Chapter 4

Build Your Dream Team

The strength of the team is each individual member. The strength of each member is the team.

–Phil Jackson

Investing in real estate is not a solo job. You will need a lot of people to come alongside you and team up in order to build a successful real estate investment opportunity for yourself. It helps to get the right input as well as the right help where needed. You will find that those who do it all themselves tend to get burned out, and they don't progress as quickly. There are experts in the field of real estate investment and in the various areas it takes to make the right decisions. Tapping into this knowledge and expertise is essential.

Putting Together the Dream Team

There are different types of people that you can contact to help you in your real estate investment journey. We are going to go through a few of these types of people. Be sure you are doing research and picking the right ones to build a relationship with.

You will likely be contacting these professionals quite often throughout your investment journey.

Accountant

Unless you are a financial wizard, an accounting professional is going to be really helpful to you. All investments involve money and finances. Accountants are people who specialize in these things. They can help you establish a financial plan so you can reach your goals. They can assist you with budgeting, investments, tax reporting, and planning. This kind of information is incredibly valuable when you are trying to make investment decisions. Ensure you pick a reliable and reputable accountant since they are handling a large part of your finances.

Agents and Broker

A real estate broker or agent is somebody who is licensed to help buy and sell property. They will be representing different parties in the purchase contract of a property. In many cases, both the buyer and the seller will have a real estate agent working with them. A real estate agent or broker will be a valuable addition to your team because they know the market and have access to different kinds of properties you might not know about. Since they are in the industry already, they have the contacts and skills needed to help you get the best deals and make the best investments.

Administrative Assistant

As you continue to grow and invest in more types of real estate, you might need to consider getting an administrative assistant. There are a lot of administrative tasks that are involved in investing and in real estate in general. Certain types of real estate investments will need more hands-on attention than others. For example, if you own an apartment block that you are renting out to tenants, it is going to take time and energy to ensure that your tenants are taken care of and that you are receiving rent from each one of them. You will need to make sure that all the bills are paid, and that maintenance has been done appropriately. An administrative assistant can take all the calls and queries from your tenants as well as ensure that the property is well looked after. All paperwork can also be handled by your assistant, and all you have to do is the most important work for your investments.

Architect

An architect is a good addition to your real estate investment team if you are looking to flip and renovate a house or property. If you are looking to build a brand-new property on vacant land, then you'll also need an architect. Not all real estate investors will need one, but it is highly dependent on what type of real estate investment you are looking to do.

Attorney

Property law can get very complicated, so it is important to have someone who understands it all. Having an attorney in your corner will make things go a lot smoother. They will be able to advise you in all the legal aspects, so you know you're not making a mistake. It is also good to have an attorney at your side just in case something were to happen with a tenant or competitor. Having someone you have a standing relationship with is typically a better option than scrambling to find a good attorney at the last minute.

Bookkeeper

Depending on how big your real estate investment business is, you might look at getting a bookkeeper. The bookkeeper can help you make decisions regarding all your finances, including budgeting. They will also assist you in keeping all your books and finances in order and assist you with keeping your financial health in a check. You can go to your bookkeeper for assistance in making decisions that regard your finances. If you already have an accountant, that might not be a reason to get a bookkeeper. However, it is a good idea to discuss with your accountant or bookkeeper what kind of services they provide and if you need an additional person.

Partner and Private Investors

If you are looking to grow your investments at a quicker pace, having partners and private investors is really helpful. You will have to ensure you are partnering up with people you actually trust; otherwise, this could turn out badly. A partner will share in the profits as well as the decision-making of your real estate investments. When it comes to investors, they will share in the profits because they are investing money in you. However, many investors do not want to be part of the decision-making process and would rather just benefit from the financial increase. It is a good idea to have a conversation with both your partners and your private investors to see what is expected from all parties involved. Contracts are also a good idea so you do not end up in an argument or fight about something that could have been easily prevented.

> It is a good idea to have a conversation with both your partners and your private investors to see what is expected from all parties involved.

Lenders

These will be companies or individual people who are willing to lend you large sums of money when you need them for investments. You will need to pay this money back in installments or in a large lump sum at a later date. You will also have to consider that there are interest rates tied to borrowing money from a lender. Having a few good and reputable lenders on your books is a great idea because it helps you make faster decisions when the time comes. Sometimes properties will be sold to those who can pay the most quickly. If you already have established relationships with a few lenders, it will be much easier for you to get the finances for your investments.

Property Manager

It is incredibly difficult to manage multiple properties all by yourself. If you are investing in actual properties and renting them out, you should consider getting a property manager. There is no need to get a property manager if you only have a few properties and are capable of handling them yourself. However, as your investments grow and you add more properties to your portfolio, you can start looking for a reputable property manager. Many property managers work for companies, and you can hire them to take care of all the day-to-day maintenance and tasks for your properties. They will make sure everything is running smoothly, and all you have to do is check in with them every now and then. Your tenants will also directly contact your property manager, so you do not have to be involved in that process either.

Marketing Coordinator

If you have a large real estate investment business, then getting a marketing coordinator is a really good idea. They will manage your brand and the presence it has in the market. They will also help to reach new businesses by finding buyers, renters, and even new properties. Building a brand is incredibly important because it leads to credibility. If you have a website or social media pages, your marketing coordinator can handle all of these for you as well.

Chapter 5

Line Up Financing

Buy land, they're not making it anymore.

–Mark Twain

Finances are a very important part of real estate investing. you will need a good amount of finances in order to invest successfully. Real estate is definitely one of the more expensive types of investing, but it also brings the most return and the most steady income. Thinking about how you will get the financing to start is one of the most important steps in your real estate investment journey.

Different Types of Loans

There are various types of loans that an individual can take when they are investing in real estate. These will depend on your situation as well as what's going to work best for you. It is always a good idea to do your research and find a loan provider that gives you the best interest-rate. Take some time to compare various products until you find the perfect one. You should always read the fine print when you are taking out a loan, as many of these can be long-term contracts, and you don't want to end up surprised down the line.

Federal Housing Administration (FHA) Loans

An FHA loan is a great option if you don't have at least 20% of the overall cost of the property for a down payment. Having the most amount of money available for your down payment is always the best option, but sometimes that might not be possible. An FHA loan allows you to purchase a property with a very small down payment. This can be as low as 3.5%. These are typically government-backed so there are definitely limits on how much you are able to borrow as well as the repayment terms. If you choose this type of property financing, you will need mortgage insurance.

Veterans Administration (VA) Loans

If you have served in any branch of the military and meet a few different requirements, you could be eligible for a Veterans Administration loan. These are also government backed and there are very strict requirements stipulating the type of property or home you are allowed to buy. These properties have to be your primary residence, and they cannot be something you were looking to fix up and flip. This does mean that it is probably not the best choice if you want to use it as an investment property. It can be very difficult to get approvals for these types of loans in this case.

Conforming Loans

The federal housing finance agency will set a dollar limit on these kinds of loans. They are typically low interest loans, so it makes them a great choice if you have a great credit score. You will have to check the updated dollar limit, as this is usually changed each year. A conforming loan can be thought of as a regular conventional loan, but there is a dollar limit to it.

Portfolio Loans

Many investors choose this type of loan when they are looking to purchase residential real estate. This type of loan is not given to another lender; it's kept in the bank or financial entities own investment portfolio. These types of loans are given to people who struggle to get other types of loans due to things like bad credit, foreclosures, and bankruptcy in the past. When you take out a typical mortgage, the bank will usually sell your loan off to a secondary lender, which is why you might have received a letter telling you to send your payments to a different address after a few months of payments. If you are the person taking out the loan, it does offer opportunities for somebody who has poor credit or is self-employed to get a loan.

Hard Money Loans

A hard money loan is also known as a bridge loan. These types of loans are for short-term borrowing that you will be able to use to help purchase your investment property. You can use this if you are house flipping or developing real estate in order to sell it in a shorter space of time. In most cases, you will need to seek out a hard money loan through a private lender, as most big financial institutions don't issue them. A hard money lender will look at the property you are looking to purchase and determine whether or not they are willing to give you the money. They will look at the value of the home after the repairs have been made and estimate how much it will be worth at that point. This type of loan is not based on your credit score or personal financial history. There are definite downsides to this type of loan, as it can be up to 10% higher than traditional loans, and the fees associated with it can also hike up the price. You also have to consider that there is a shorter repayment. So unless you know you will make your money back really quickly, this is not going to be a great choice for you.

Private Lenders

A private lender is an institution or a person that will issue a loan that will be secured by a trust deed. Typically, you will need to have a relationship with the person you are looking to borrow money from. Since these are non-institutional lenders, the loans can be seen as short-term in most cases. The individual or entity you are taking a loan from will determine the conditions and rules surrounding it. It is always wise to sign a contract when you use a private lender so that everybody is clear on what the rules and expectations are.

Seller Financing

Seller financing takes place when the seller of the property agrees for the buyer to pay for the property in instalments. In this case, the seller does not get all of the money at once. In order to go this route, you will have to find a seller who is willing to do so. There are many sellers who prefer the traditional route because they want all of their money upfront. There is no guarantee that you'll find a seller who is willing to do this, so unless you have worked out a previous agreement with the current property owner, you shouldn't expect this to be a viable option. You can always ask and set the terms, but it will ultimately be up to the seller.

Chapter 6

Start Your Journey

Success in real estate starts when you believe you are worthy of it.

–Michael Ferrara

We all need to start somewhere. Sometimes it is the beginning of a journey that gets us stumped. This is actually quite common because the destination might seem really far away. If you flip your mentality and decide to take it one day at a time, then it actually becomes more exciting. Investing, like much of life, is not about being an expert from the get-go. It is about being willing to make changes as necessary.

This chapter is going to be about the start of your journey. It is going to take you through a few of the steps you need to take in order to get started. If you start taking action as soon as possible, you will be able to continue on with that momentum. This is going to make it easier for you to keep going. The sooner you start, the sooner you will see results.

Identify Your Financial Stage

You will need to discover what your financial stage is. This will determine how much you can afford to invest in real estate. You can think of your finances as the platform that will allow everything else to take off. At the end of the day, you will need to have some sort of capital to work with. The more you have access to, the more you will be able to invest, and the faster your investments can grow and bring in a profit.

There are typically two starting points for real estate investors. The first one is not having any money but looking to plan for your future investments. The second is having a large sum of money to invest but not knowing how to do so. Depending on where you start, your next move will be determined. Let's first talk about the first scenario. If you do not have the funds to invest just yet, you are in a great position to start planning. Your next move will be to think about how you would like to invest in real estate and then move on to setting realistic goals for yourself. If you are looking to purchase a property, you would need a good amount saved up for a down payment. If investing in REITs is what you are looking into, you might only need to rework your budget to help free up some money to invest. Once you have your goals set in place, you will then take the steps necessary to reach them.

> If you do not have the funds to invest just yet, you are in a great position to start planning.

If you already have the money to invest but are not sure what the next step is, you need to get the research done. One of the biggest mistakes people make when they already have the cash, they need is to make impulsive investments. While it is important to start investing as soon as you can, you still need to take some time to research and make a good choice. You want to see the benefits of investing in the shortest time frame possible, and you definitely don't want to waste your investment capital by making a bad purchase. The rest of the chapter is going to help you make a better choice when it comes to investing in real estate. You can set a target date for your final decision, so you do not procrastinate, but make sure you have set aside enough time to research and think about it.

Pick a Target Market

Picking a target market is really going to help you choose a property to invest in. Since there are so many different types of real estate investments, you need to make sure the target market is going to be catered to. If you already have a vision for how you want your property to be used, it will help you narrow down your options. It can feel overwhelming to go on the hunt for the perfect property. The options are endless. Not knowing your target audience or the type of investment you are making allows you to run the risk of buying something that does not bring in the profit you hoped for. You will also be limited in what you can do if you buy a property without planning it out.

Let's say you want to purchase a property to rent out to someone on a long-term basis. This property will need to meet certain criteria in order to be appealing to the type of person you want to attract. As an example, your perfect tenants would be a couple who do not have kids. In this case, you would start thinking about what this type of person would need out of their home. They would likely want one or two-bedrooms, be close to transportation, be close to the city for work purposes, be close to good restaurants and bars, and have a few amenities close by.

Using this criteria, you are able to narrow down your search to find the perfect townhouse or apartment for your ideal tenants. You would first start by finding a few locations that suit their needs, and then you could look for properties that fit the bill within those locations. When it comes time to market your property, you will be able to highlight all of these key factors and state why it would be perfect for a young, career minded couple.

If your target market is a family with kids who are looking for a place to spend the week on vacation, the above property would not appeal to them. You would need to change up your criteria and plan going forward. Instead of just one or two-bedrooms, you are looking at three or more. You would also need to look for a place that is near tourist attractions and activities that kids would enjoy. Finding a house or an apartment close to the beach might be a better option for this group of people. You would market your property in such a way to attract them.

This is not to say that if you pick a target market, you are actively closing yourself off to other types of people and customers. You will notice that you might attract people who are not in your target market. This is pretty common. The goal of choosing a target market is to help you narrow your strategy and ensure you are catering to the needs of a specific group. When you try to be too general, you end up missing the mark on all counts, and this will result in you making a smaller profit than desired.

Evaluate Big Picture Location Criteria

Location is definitely one of the most important things to consider when investing in real estate. You could have the most beautiful house that has all brand-new and trendy finishes, but if it is not in the right location people will not want to go there. Most people would prefer to stay on a mediocre property in an amazing location, than in a five-star property that is in the middle of nowhere. There are many different factors to think about when it comes to location. We are going to go through them so you are well equipped when looking for your next real estate investment.

Jobs and Economics

This might sound like a strange thing to consider when it comes to property location, but the economy of an area is telling of its potential growth. When you are investing in a property, you need to make sure that the value will increase year over year. Purchasing a property in a city with a dying economy is a recipe for a depreciating asset. People are drawn to a city or town because there are job opportunities there.

A good way to figure out whether or not a location is growing and creating jobs is to drive through it. If you notice there is construction taking place and the city or town is lively, this is a good sign. If you notice there are tons of empty businesses and lots, along with the area not being well taken care of, chances are that this is not the location for you. You can do some internet research as well. Simply typing in the name of the surrounding area and seeing what pops up can give you a few clues. You will be able to see any new developments that are taking place and the future plans for the area. Take a peek at the local municipalities' website and see if you can get some information there. You can also go onto a job posting website and see how many jobs are being advertised in that location. All of this will help you make a more informed choice.

Population Growth

Economic growth will bring about population growth as more people will be attracted to the area. You should have a look at the population statistics in the area. This is typically found on the local government website. You will be able to see if there is steady population growth in the area or if it is declining. Take some time to figure out what is driving the growth or decline. The birth of new babies in the area is definitely not the only contributing factor to population growth. Perhaps this area is known for its good weather, and there has been investment in social activities in the area. In this case, it might attract new retirees who want to enjoy their golden years.

Knowing why population growth is taking place will help you decide whether or not your target market will enjoy the area. Beware of sudden spikes in population. This might seem like a good thing, but it can often be unsustainable. The draw to the area might just be short-term and investing in a property could end up losing you money if the thing that attracts people fizzles out.

Rent/Price Ratio

Taking some time to find out how much people are willing to pay for rent or nightly rates in the area is important. You need to make sure the amount you are paying for the property will pay off down the line. The goal is to make your money back as soon as you can. Checking out the competition will really help you with this. If you are planning on renting out your property long-term, it is a good idea to go onto a local property website. Look for a property that is very similar to yours and see how much the owners are charging for rent. Try and find more than one example so you can get a better general idea. Find out how long each property has been on the market so you can gauge whether people are actually willing to pay that price or not. A good sign that a property is overpriced or does not offer what people are looking for is if it has been on the market for a number of months.

If you are looking to use your property as a holiday rental, you can look at sites like Airbnb to see what the going rate is. Utilize the filters so you find properties in your location that offer similar amenities and space. Remember, when looking at the rental prices on sites like Airbnb, don't forget to look at the occupancy rates. If they're asking very high prices, it can look very promising, but if they're not booked out, then clearly potential guests do not feel the price is justified. You can also take some tips from these successful properties and replicate what they do in your own way. Have a look at what they offer and how they market the property. It is definitely not a good idea to directly copy them, but you can use them for inspiration.

Once you fully understand what people are willing to pay for a property like yours, you can start thinking about what you are willing to pay for a mortgage. You should aim to make enough to at least cover the mortgage payments each month. If you feel comfortable with the ratio, then you can go ahead and make an offer. If not, see if the current property owner is willing to negotiate with you for a better price.

Evaluate Small Scale Location Criteria

The above was all about the large-scale criteria you should be on the lookout for. Once you have that all sorted, it is time to move onto the smaller things. Chances are, you are not going to find the absolute best property that ticks all the boxes. There will be some compromises needed. However, the goal is to get as close as possible to perfection. You can also make a list of priorities, so you know that the things at the top of the list are non-negotiable but the ones at the bottom allow for some wiggle room.

Convenience

The convenience factor is important to both you and your potential tenants. If you are managing your property on your own, then you would need to ensure you can get to and from your new property with ease. If you buy a property two hours away from where you live, you will have a two-hour commute every time you need to attend to something. When you have people staying on your property, you will be the one they call if they need assistance. Buying a property that is convenient to get to will save you a lot of trouble in the long run.

> If you are managing your property on your own, then you would need to ensure you can get to and from your new property with ease.

If you are able to hire someone to manage your property for you, then you do not have to worry about this. The management company will take care of everything for you, and you can enjoy a passive form of income. However, there is a fee you would need to pay, so take this into consideration. You will need to work this into your overall rent change or your nightly rate. Buying a property that will incur these extra costs to run needs to be worth it. You would need to do some research to find out whether you will be able to charge this inflated price in a given area.

Romance

If you are planning on renting out your property for holiday-goers, a romantic feel is always a winner. Couples are always on the lookout for a romantic setting, and it is a big draw if you can provide that. This doesn't mean you have to paint your house red and plant roses all over the lawn. Romance can be subtle and classy. This way, you will also be able to cater for other types of guests who are checking into your rental.

Romance is also in the type of location in which your property is situated. Beach houses, cabins, and villas all have something romantic about them, and you can use this as a selling point. If your property is located in an area, then make sure to play this up. You can carry the romance from the outside into the actual property as well. Look out for romantic restaurants and activities around your potential property investment.

Walkability

Walkability is exactly what it sounds like. You are judging how easy it is to get around by walking. Amenities would be close by, and the streets would be clean and easy to navigate. Some areas are simply not meant for tourists or the average person to walk about, and this can be a big drawback. Walkability is important for both long-term and short-term rentals, as people might want to get around without the use of traditional transport.

The best way to find out the walkability of an area is to go for a walk there. Take a drive to your desired neighborhood and walk around for as long as you can. Try to go through various streets and experience as much as you can. You can make note of how long it takes to walk to certain amenities and also about the overall experience. This is great information if you are planning on renting out your property, as you can use it to market your property. The more you understand your investment, the better.

Safety and Crime Rates

It is easy to find the crime rates of a city by simply searching online for them. The government website should have all the information you need. It goes without saying that you should be on the lookout for areas with low crime rates. The more crime that takes place in an area, the less likely people are to want to live there. You will have to significantly drop your prices to attract people to a high crime location. Properties that are situated in areas that are not safe also have a higher chance of being broken into and damaged. You can expect additional costs to fix damages and replace stolen goods.

School Districts

Families with children will be looking at school districts when making their decisions. This is not a big deal if you are renting out your property to holiday goers, but if you are renting it out long-term or are looking to flip and sell, then taking this into consideration is a good idea. A good school district could help you bump up the price of your property.

Public Transportation

Not everyone has cars or wants to use their own transportation all the time. This is why public transportation is important. Your property should be close to bus stops and easily accessible to other forms of public transport. Your vacation guests will also appreciate this, as many of them would prefer not to be behind the wheel while they are on vacation. Make sure to highlight the type of public transportation available to them.

Neighborhood Covenants and HOAs

HOA stands for homeowners association. Certain areas will have these in place to enforce a set of rules to make the area ideal for all who live there. This could be a good thing for you or could work against you. Certain HOAs are not fond of short-term and holiday rentals in their area, and this could make it difficult to establish yourself there. It is best to find out the rules of the area and ensure you are able to meet them should you purchase there. You will need to sign something with them agreeing to the terms before you can join. HOAs are not all bad. You will be paying a fee, and there are many perks that are included, such as trash removal, lawn care, and use of recreational areas. Each one will be different, so you will need to find out exactly what you are paying for.

Chapter 7

Marketing and Expansion

The bottom line: investing in real estate is smart because property is tangible. People always have, and always will, need shelter. This means it is very unlikely that our need for shelter (ie: buying or renting homes) will ever go away.

–Kathy Fettke

Marketing is going to be the backbone of your investment. This goes for almost all types of direct real estate investing. You should have space in your budget for marketing, and you should be realistic about it. There are definitely ways you can market yourself on the cheaper end, but you might need a bit more help, which is why having enough funds allocated is important. You could try out the cheaper options first and see if they yield the results you want. If not, you can go for the pricer options.

Free and Low-Cost Options

The great thing about marketing is that you don't always have to go for the most expensive options. There are tons of marketing tactics that are cheap or even free. We will be going through some of these options in this section. You do not have to implement all of them. Marketing is meant to be sustainable, so choose the ones that will work best for you and bring about the most results.

Social Media

Using social media to your advantage can help you expand your reach among your target audience. There are very few people who aren't on social media, so you will definitely be able to find the right people here. The trick is to use the right social media for the type of audience you are trying to reach. Look at your target demographic and do some research to see which is their preferred social media platform. For example, older people tend to be on Facebook, but very few people in their early 20s are on Facebook consistently. TikTok and Instagram are platforms that will be great for reaching people from younger generations.

With this being said, you might want to consider creating a page for each social media platform. This way, you can increase your reach. Instagram and Facebook can be linked, so you can post on one and it will automatically be shared on the other. Creating TikTok content will take a bit more effort, as you will need to film and edit short videos. You can share these on Instagram and Facebook as well. Try to let your creativity flow with this and just have some fun. It can seem daunting at first, but consistency is key. The more consistent you are, the more likely you are to be seen. Make sure all the content you post is real estate or property specific so you can get the right audience interested in your content and your properties.

Referral and Networking Campaign

A great way to get people to buy into what you are doing is through referrals. Most people are skeptical of something new, but if a trusted person backs it up, it will seem more credible. This is why many brands partner up with influencers to show off their items. People are more likely to buy something when there is a trusted source endorsing it. You don't have to spend thousands of dollars to get influencers to market your property; you just have to get people to share and refer you to others.

Offering incentives for people to share your social media content or your other marketing avenues will get people to talk to their friends about you. This is especially important if you run a short-term rental. I have seen many different types of referral marketing strategies put in place. A way to get the ball rolling is to offer someone a free stay at your vacation rental if they are willing to post about it on social media and share it with others. This is fairly cheap, and it will get the ball rolling. As soon as you start getting the word out there, you will see more and more people becoming interested.

You could also run a competition on your social media pages. You have probably seen many brands and companies do this. All you have to do is create an enticing prize, such as an all-expenses paid weekend stay at your rental. In order to enter, people will need to tag a certain number of friends as well as share it on their social media stories. People go crazy for free things, and you will get the word out there quite quickly. The more people who are aware of your property, the more likely you are to get the right people to book with you.

Cold Calls

Most people don't like doing cold calling, but there is a reason why many businesses still do it… it works! You will have to perfect your sales pitch so you can get people interested. You will also have to accept the fact that rejection comes with the territory. You could make a hundred calls and only get one or two people interested in what you have to say. Depending on the type of real estate investing you are taking part in, you will tailor your pitch to match. Remember to ask each person you call for the number of someone they believe would be interested in what you are offering. It is also best to use a separate phone number to make the calls, as you don't want all of these people to have your private number.

Classified Ads

Classified ads are still a thing! Many newspapers have physical copies still being sold, and they have online platforms. You can pay a small fee to get the newspaper, magazine, or online site to publish your ad. Back in the day, classified ads were the only way to get the word out there, and they were very effective. Chances are, you will be targeting the older generation with these, as most people under the age of 30 will not be reading these sources.

Intermediate and High-Cost Options

If you want to kick things up a notch, you can try these higher priced options. These are more effective, but you will be forking out a bit more money on them. It is a good idea to have a marketing budget, so you know how much you are able to spend. After a few months, you can check to see how effective each strategy has been for you. Keep the ones that are working and cut the rest.

Email

Email is still one of the best ways to connect with potential customers and buyers. Most companies are still taking part in email marketing, regardless of the demographics of their target audience. In order to do this effectively, you will need to sign up with an email marketing service such as Mailchimp. You will be sending emails to potential customers and buyers about deals, specials, news, and tips and tricks. This can take some time because you want to produce content that gets people interested. It is important to be as consistent as possible. You never know which email will be the one that gets people interested. Be aware that many people won't even open your emails, and this is pretty normal. The average person does not open every email from those they are subscribed to. However, you will be surprised at how many people read and engage with their emails.

Website

Creating a website for your real estate investment business is a really good idea. It will help you to create a brand for yourself. If you are planning on having more than one property, then this is going to help people find properties that are owned by you. They will be able to see your mission and vision for the future as well as any present endeavors. It establishes trust when you have an online presence, and the chances of you getting more people interested in what you do are higher.

There are costs associated with running a website. First of all, you will need to purchase a domain name. This is what people will be typing into the browser in order to be taken to your website. Domain names can be tricky because you want to pick one that is easy to remember and still speaks to your business. Since a website is part of your brand, you need to make sure it matches up to the rest of your marketing and advertising efforts. It is a good idea to pick a name for your investment business, and then you can use this name as part of your domain name. There are already so many websites out there that it might take some time to find an available domain name. You will have to try out a few combinations before you find one that you like and that is available. There are domain name generators that you can use to help. These are typically free, and all you have to do is type in a few criteria and look at the options.

Once you have landed on your domain name, lock it in as quickly as possible. Domain names can get scooped up fast, so once you find one you are happy with, purchase it so you can avoid disappointment. You can always let the license expire if you realize there is a better option. Choosing the right domain name is also good for website SEO. SEO stands for "search engine optimization." This helps people find you when they are searching for something on the web. Everything you do on your website should be optimized in this way. This means you will have to use relevant keywords in all your posts and content on the website. This will really help people stumble upon your website and will be beneficial to your overall marketing strategy.

If you do not have the time or expertise to handle your website on your own, you can look to outsource this. Websites do require work to keep them up and running. There are dozens of hosting services that make things a lot easier for you. Using one of these will allow all the costs to be rolled into one, but you do have to keep in mind that there are restrictions on the type of website you can build. Everything will need to be done according to a template that works with the hosting service. If you choose to host your website yourself, you will need to ensure you have the resources to take care of it and keep it updated. Websites require consistency, so carve out some time for them or hire someone to take care of your website for you.

Car Signs

I'm sure you have seen cars that look like moving advertisements on the road. This is an effective way to get your name out there in your city. It will help you catch the eye of relevant people. There are websites you can sign up on where you can find someone who is willing to wrap their car in your advertisement. This will come at a cost, but the platform will ensure the cars used are up to standard. Before someone applies to wrap their car, it needs to meet a few criteria. This includes driving a certain distance per week and having a car that is neat and clean. You will need to have your advertisement signed to fit on the car, and make sure that the contact details are visible to people who drive by.

Yard Signs

Most people in the property business have invested in some

kind of yard sign. The most common types are the ones you find outside the house of someone trying to sell. Usually, it is the real estate company that has these signs all over. You can also create these signs and post them outside the houses and properties you are selling or flipping. Yard signs are a great way to notify people in the area that something is happening with a certain property you are working on.

Advertising

There are various traditional advertising methods you can use. Many of these will come at a cost that needs to be budgeted for. If you do not have a large budget for advertising, then some of these can be out of reach. However, it is good to think about the future. When you are more established in your investing journey, you will be able to look into these ways. The reason these things cost a bit more is because they do take more effort and often yield better results.

You could consider creating video advertisements that you publish on your social media platforms and use on social media ad campaigns. Platforms like Facebook and YouTube will run your ads for a price. Social media platforms offer a unique opportunity in advertising. Back in the day, the only way to do video ads was on the TV. These were really effective, but the problem is that the ads would be shared with everyone watching and not be targeted to a specific group. This means you would have to pay a large amount and not have any guarantee that your ad will be seen by the right person. With social media ads, you will be able to choose the demographic of people you want to reach, and your ads will only be shown to those groups. This means your money will be better put to use, and you will likely see better results.

The budget for this type of advertisement also has to take into account the creation of the ads. You might need to hire some professionals to write and film your ad campaign if you are unable to do it yourself. If you do not have any connections in this space, consider hiring a freelancer. You will be able to get an excellent end product, but the pricing will likely be lower than a professional cast and crew.

Another traditional form of advertising would be billboards and posters. You will have to get in touch with the relevant parties so you can use this advertising space. You might also look into radio advertisements. You could either have the radio presenters speak about you or you could create an audio ad that gets played to the audience. As you can see, there are various types of traditional advertising that you could consider. Phone around so you are able to get the best price.

Chapter 8

Analyzing Property

Real estate cannot be lost or stolen, nor can it be carried away. Purchased with common sense, paid for in full, and managed with reasonable care, it is about the safest investment in the world.

–Franklin D. Roosevelt

A property will likely be the biggest investment of your life. There are very few things that cost as much and end up making as much money as property has the potential of doing. This is why it is essential to make the right choice. You want to be able to set yourself up for success. This means property analysis is crucial. You need to ensure that you know where you are putting your money. Some people decide to skip the analysis, but this is a huge mistake. We are going to be talking more about this topic in this chapter.

> You need to ensure that you know where you are putting your money. Some people decide to skip the analysis, but this is a huge mistake.

Things to Be Considered When Analyzing

There are a variety of things that need to be considered when you are analyzing a potential investment property. These should be done separately, and then you can look at everything as a whole. Analysis can take some time, so be aware of this. It is not something you can get finished up in a few minutes. When you do this properly you will be able to make better predictions of how your property will perform. This will also help you make better choices about the type of property you are going to invest in. On top of this, you should also perform analysis on properties you already own. This will help you discover whether or not your properties are performing the way you need them to. If there are changes that need to be made, you can take care of them as early as possible.

The Physical Property

You will need to perform some analysis on the physical property and its characteristics. There are quite a few things to consider here, and it is essential that you do this right. You will be performing this kind of analysis when you have found a property you are interested in. The one part of the analysis that we are not going to be talking about is location, since we have spoken about it in later chapters. This should be done before you settle on a property.

When you are looking to invest in a property, you will need to consider the infrastructure of the actual property. You need to make sure that it is up to code and that there isn't going to be a lot you need to do. If you are planning on buying a cheap property and then renovating it, you can be a bit more lenient with this. Just make sure you know what you are getting into. Many people who try to get rid of their houses will hide certain things about them. This is not ethical, but it does happen. This is why you need to make sure you do not just take things on the word of the current owners. A proper inspection is critical, as is asking for all the relevant papers from the current owners. You can also get a professional to do an evaluation for you. This will need to be cleared by the current owners, and it will come at a cost to you.

The inspection should be as thorough as possible. You will need to look out for any visible signs of damage that could cause problems later on. Mold, heating, electrical faults, and plumbing issues can all be huge costs down the line, and you don't want to deal with that. When you are inspecting the property, you should get a good idea of what needs to be done before you can make a profit on it. This could change depending on the type of investment you are making. Be sure to ask the current owners and the real estate agents as many questions as possible. This should give you a better overall idea of the property.

Environmental Analysis

When it comes to property, the environment can cause things to take place that are out of your control. This could mean losing out on your investment because Mother Nature decided not to play nice. Doing some research on the environmental factors at play is a really good idea. You will first need to look at the weather in that area to determine whether or not it is prone to natural disasters. This will play a role in what you can use the property for. If you are looking to rent out a property as a holiday rental, the weather is important. People typically don't go on vacation to areas that have unpredictable weather conditions unless there are other big draws to the area.

When it comes to weather, you will need to make sure the property you choose can withstand the types of conditions Mother Nature puts forward. If the area is particularly wet and rainy, the property you invest in will need to have drainage and preferably not be surrounded by soft ground. You should be on the lookout for a property that is not sunken, as rain water can pool up and make things very inconvenient. These things will need to be done when you are doing an analysis on the physical property, but you will need to know the weather conditions and risks before you know what characteristics the property needs.

Environmental analysis is not just about natural occurrences. You can consider anything external to the property. Changes that are taking place in the community could also play a huge role in determining whether or not a specific property will be a good buy. Take a look at the property laws and any other national laws that could affect a specific area. You don't want to be caught off guard later down the line. A shift in demographics is another thing you want to pay attention to. If the town is getting older, younger, or has an increase in a certain group of people (such as retirees, university students, or business professionals), this could all have an impact on how your property does.

Market Analysis

A market analysis will show you how much you can expect to pay for your property as well as how much you will be making from it based on the type of investing you are doing. It is essential to do this type of research so you can prepare yourself well and ensure that you are going to be getting the best prices in all regards. If you are using a real estate agent, they might put together some numbers for you. This is an important tool, but you should also do some of your own research. You should be able to trust your agent, but you never know, and it is better to be safe than sorry.

Real estate agents typically do property valuations, where they price the home based on the current market. If you are looking to sell a home, they will tell you how much you can expect to get for it. However, if you are looking to buy a property, the goal of many real estate agents will be to sell it for the highest price. This means you might not get the best price. Having some base knowledge of the general pricing in the area as well as for a similar property will be really helpful. You have some base knowledge, so you will be able to negotiate and counter correctly. You can also go online and do some research to get the estimated value of the home. If many real estate agents are working on the same property, you will likely find there is a difference in pricing for the same property. When doing online research, it is important to note that it might not be completely accurate. If there were changes and renovations done to the home, the pricing might go up. Take this into consideration when you are doing some market research.

There will likely be a few properties that are similar to the one you have your eye on in the same area. Finding out how much these are going for will help you understand whether you are overpaying for yours. Checking out some property listing websites will be helpful. In order to find similar properties, all you have to do is click the filters that apply to your property, and others that meet the same criteria will pop up. There are many things that could increase the price of the house, including the number of rooms, parking garages, a pool, and renovations. This is why it is important to get as close to your property as possible when trying to make comparisons.

If you are house flipping or looking to sell the property relatively quickly after you have purchased it, then you need to look at the buying and selling data in that area. You don't want to purchase a property only to struggle to get it sold. Certain times of the year or market conditions could result in being able to sell. In these cases, you might have to adjust your strategy. For example, in a recession it is common for houses and other property to sell for quite cheap. This is because people can no longer afford to live in their current properties and need to sell quickly. On top of that, people are not really buying because things are tight. It can be a good strategy to buy during a recession, but you should not expect to sell immediately and make a profit. This situation would be a buy and hold type of investment. If you have the time to wait for the market to pick up again, then you can wait and make a large profit in a few years. The type of investment you are trying to make will influence whether or not it is a good time to invest.

Another aspect of the market you will need to do some research on is your competition. Knowing what you are up against is essential when you are renting out your property. You need to see what your property will likely go for and what others are offering. There is always competition, and it is actually better to enter an already existing market than start one from scratch. This means that it is actually a good sign if there are successful properties in your area. It shows that people are looking to rent and are willing to pay. This is regardless of whether you are planning on renting out your property long-term or for vacation rentals. Just make sure you are comparing properties that are doing the same thing. If you notice there are a lot of properties being rented out in an area, but they are staying vacant, this is an indication that the market is just not there. You might have to rethink your location and find somewhere that is more in demand.

Potential Income

When you are making an investment, income is important. This is if you have chosen an investment method that does bring in an income instead of a lump sum of money. Thinking about the income before you purchase the property will help you decide whether or not the property is actually worth it. You don't want to make a purchase only to realize that you spent way too much or that it was a bad purchase.

The way you calculate how much you could potentially make will depend on the type of real estate investment strategy you are pursuing. Let's go through a few of them so you get a better idea. Let's start with vacation rental properties. These have the potential to make you the most money, but they also carry a certain amount of risk. There is no guarantee that your property will be booked out at all times. If your property is not being booked out, it means you are not making money at those times. With this being said, if your financial strategy is good then you don't have to have a continuously booked out vacation rental.

In fact, an occupancy rate of around 60% is incredibly successful, and most people don't even get there. If you are able to get a 30–50% occupancy rate, then you are in a good place. The occupancy rate is the number of days your property is booked out in relation to the number of available days. When it comes to vacation rentals or short-term rentals in general, the weekends will be the most common time for bookings. Depending on where your property is situated, you might only get weekend bookings. This will result in your occupancy rate being really low since only two or three nights are being booked in the week, but this does not mean you are unsuccessful.

You should also consider how much you will be charging per night. Going on a platform like Airbnb will help you see what others are charging for a similar stay. You can then get a realistic idea of what you can charge. You might also notice that there are different prices for different days of the week and times of the year. This is a normal strategy that vacation rental owners use. Prices to stay over the weekend will be higher as this is a more in demand time of the week and people are willing to pay a little extra. During the week, prices are dropped slightly to encourage people to book at non-peak times. The same logic follows times of the year. There are certain times of the year when your area will be in demand as a holiday destination.

Let's say your property is in a coastal region. People will likely book with you more often in the summer so they can enjoy the beaches. This means your high season will be in the warmer months. You would be able to charge more because your property is in demand. During the winter, you will have to drop your prices in order to make your property more attractive and offer a better deal than your competitors. Even with this strategy, low seasons are common, and you should expect less occupancy at this time. Take all of this into consideration when you are planning your potential income. It will never be perfect, but you should be as realistic as possible when doing this. It will help you plan and prepare for the type of property you are looking to purchase.

Another scenario would be if you were planning to use your property as a long-term rental. This strategy makes it a lot easier to plan your potential income. All you have to do is find out how much people are willing to pay to rent out your property. Looking at property websites will give you a good idea of this. Long-term rental income can be predicted a lot easier than short-term rental income. This is because you will be charging a certain amount for rent each month. There are contracts in place to make the tenant responsible for this amount, and the income will be steady for as long as you have someone living in the property. Maintenance and turnover costs will also be lower since you do not have to ensure the property is clean and ready each time there is a new guest, as with a short-term rental. You also might not have to buy furniture and decor since people will likely bring them. If you fully furnish the property, you will be able to charge more to rent it out.

Regardless of the type of property investing you are planning on doing, there will be some expenses. It is important to not overlook these when you are planning your total income. The money that comes in is not all going to be profit. You will need to pay bills and make sure the property is up to scratch before you can work out your profit. Take some time to think of the recurring payments you will need to make so you can get a realistic idea of what your profit will be.

Development Costs

In most cases, you will have to do some work on the property before you can put it on the market and make some money. This comes at a cost, and it is a good idea to have an estimate before you get started. A big mistake that people make is that they simply think about purchasing the property and do nothing after that. The purchase of the property will be the largest expense, but there are other costs. If the property is a fixer-upper, then you will need to have a budget in place for what needs to be done and the costs involved. Large-scale renovations will be expensive, so you need to know how much you can afford in total. This way, you can buy a property that will be priced reasonably enough for you to have the money for these improvements.

> A big mistake that people make is that they simply think about purchasing the property and do nothing after that.

If you have done a proper property analysis, you will also have a good idea of what needs to be done to the property. Perhaps the house needs some new plumbing or the paint job is looking a bit old. When doing the analysis, make sure you take note of all the things that need to be done. These need to be worked into your budget before you make an offer on the property. Understanding all the costs involved will help you plan out your finances in a more realistic manner.

Other costs also need to be considered later on down the line. If you are renting your property out as a vacation rental, then you need to understand the costs that come with this. While you can make a lot of money through this method of property investing, you also have to understand that it comes with a few continuous costs. When running a vacation rental your job is to ensure that your guests have the best experience possible. This means providing them with the necessities for their stay.

If you think about when you stay in a hotel or a vacation home, there are things provided for you. Towels, linen, bath products, utensils, cleaning products, toilet paper, toiletries, and condiments are typically found. These things cost money. For linens and towels, you will need to make sure these are cleaned before every guest. For many of the other products, these will have to be replaced by new guests. These need to be planned within your budget, as they are a necessity. These might not fall under "developmental costs," but they are important costs to consider nonetheless.

Chapter 9

Maintenance of Property

Owning a home is a keystone of wealth…both financial affluence and emotional security.

–Suze Orman

Once you have your property, the hard work is not done. Properties are managed, and this is a continuous thing. With this being said, there are things that can be done to lessen the burden. We will be going over all of these in this chapter. It is always a good idea to be prepared for the maintenance that comes with a property. You don't want to be shocked at the work and money required once you have already made the purchase.

Using Preventative Property Maintenance

One of the best things you can do for your property is preventive property maintenance. This is when you make sure things are running smoothly and are in good condition. This will help prevent any bigger issues down the line. It is easy to sweep the little things under the rug, but you will end up paying for them later on, and the bill is not going to be cheap. This is why it is always better to prevent any issues than wait for them to occur. If you have a rental property, this is even more important. It becomes a safety issue when people are living on your property. If someone gets injured, then this could easily turn into a lawsuit, and I'm sure you do not want to deal with that.

You should plan to do preventive property maintenance once a year so you can get ahead of any problems. If you have tenants living in your property, make sure they are aware that this will be taking place at a stipulated time and date. Below is a list of the things you will need to check during your inspections. This is actually also good practice for the home you are living in. Making this a habit will save you a lot of headaches.

Pests

Pests can cause a lot of trouble in a home, so make sure you are looking out for them. Doing a once over to ensure there aren't any pests is a good practice. If you live in an area that is prone to pests, you might want to spray every year to ensure they do not make a home on your property.

Water Damage and Plumbing

Take some time to look at all the visible plumbing on your property. All the pipes, taps, and fixtures should be working properly, and there shouldn't be any leaks. You should also look out for water damage, as this is a sign of a leak somewhere. Water damage can easily be ignored, but it can lead to mold and other larger problems if it is not dealt with. The caulk and grout should also be looked at, as these things can wear over time and then be prone to water damage.

Walls and Ceilings

Have a look to see if you can spot any cracks or damage to these areas. This is essential to the look and safety of the house. A small crack can turn into a big problem down the line. It might also be a sign of a larger problem.

Filters

If you have air conditioners and heaters, the filters will need to be replaced regularly. This is an often-overlooked step, but it can lead to bad air quality as well as damage to the machine.

Roof and Gutters

Take some time to look at the roof to see if all the shingles are secure and that there is no major damage to the roof. Roof damage could lead to water leaks if there is a storm, so you do want to check thoroughly. While you are up there, have a look at the gutters. These can back up quite quickly and cause problems. Take some time to sort this out if there is a problem.

Check the Detectors

Smoke and carbon monoxide detectors are important tools for keeping people safe. If the batteries run out or they stop working, this could lead to injury and illness. A quick check is essential.

If you are not available or do not want to do these kinds of checks and inspections, you can hire a professional to do them.

You will get a certificate, and this can be shown to your tenants. If you are working with a property management company, they will likely handle all this for you and make the workload lighter.

Insurance of Your Property

After you have made a huge purchase, you need to protect it. This is where insurance comes in. I have witnessed many property investors and owners take chances and not take out insurance. The truth is, most of them end up regretting it. You will need to pay insurance premiums, but this is nothing compared to having to pay out a lump sum due to an unforeseen circumstance. Not having insurance might lead you into debt or result in you having to sell your property because you can't afford to fix whatever happened.

The most important thing to note is that regular homeowners insurance might not be enough for you as a property investor. There are definitely certain aspects that are the same, but you will need a bit more to make sure you are fully covered. Depending on the type of investing you are doing, you might want to look into landlords' insurance. This covers everything traditional homeowners insurance covers, but it will also cover your liability if the tenant causes harm or damage to the property or if the tenant is injured on your property. This is useful if you happen to find yourself in a lawsuit laid out by a tenant due to an accident.

It is always a good idea to have a look at your insurance coverage to see what is included. Certain service providers might have more or less options available. You will also need to look at your specific situation and decide what is necessary based on that. Some types of insurance might not be applicable to you, and others will. Even though insurance is really important, you don't want to be paying more than you have to. For example, if your property is in a coastal region or one that is prone to natural disasters, you will need to get insurance that covers flood or hurricane damage. However, someone with the same type of property as you that is situated inland with no risk of these things will not need the coverage. This is why it is important to do your property analysis correctly so you know what you need and what you can skip out on. As a property investor, there will be a few types of insurance that are highly advised. There are hazards and fires, liability, loss of income, and rent guarantee insurance. These will help protect your investment and ensure that you are covered in the event of a loss of income. A few others you can consider are flood and water damage, workers' compensation (if you have staff on the property), sewer and water backup, and an umbrella policy.

> As a property investor, there will be a few types of insurance that are highly advised. There are hazards and fires, liability, loss of income, and rent guarantee insurance.

Adding Value to Your Property (Renovation)

Adding to your property will result in more income in various ways. If you are flipping the property, renovations are necessary. You can increase the price you sell your home for by a large amount by making the right renovations. Now, it is important to understand that an increase in value is not guaranteed. It really depends on the market and the type of renovations you make. Some of them are more expensive than others so make sure you have done the necessary research before you dive in.

Curb-Side Appeal

Curb-side appeal should never be underestimated. How many times have you driven by a really stunning property and wished you could live there? The outside is what draws you in. You don't even know what the inside looks like, but you already find yourself wishing for a home like that. If you are using your property as a vacation rental, the first impression also really matters. You will be able to charge more if you have made improvements to the outside of the home.

The great thing about this is you don't have to spend an arm and a leg in order to increase the value. First off, you will have to make sure the yard is well taken care of, if you have one. Get a gardener in to help you trim the bushes and cut the grass. You can add something extra with a few plants and do a little landscaping if needed. Another thing that can transform the property is a fresh coat of paint. It can make a home look brand-new, and it isn't very expensive. Try to stick with classic colors rather than really loud and bright ones. These do stand out, but you will be walking a very thin line to tacky. That is not a look that will add value. If you are unsure of what color you should paint your house, going for white or off-white is usually a safe bet. You can add some dimension by using a different color for the trimmings.

Add to the Kitchen

The two biggest drawcards of a home are the kitchen and the bathrooms. This could make or break the value of the home, so make sure you spend some time here. The kitchen is essential because people spend a lot of time here and they want it to be functional. Even if you have a vacation rental, you still want the kitchen to be functional and easy to work in. People who stay in these kinds of rentals might choose to stay longer and will need access to a kitchen if they do not want to eat out every day.

There are many things you can do to a kitchen that can add value, but adding a kitchen island and a pantry will serve you best in terms of adding value. This is especially true when you have people living in the house permanently or for a long period of time. A kitchen island is a modern touch to a kitchen, and it gives more workspace. On top of that, you can add some seating, so it becomes a place for the family and friends to sit together and enjoy some good food. A walk-in pantry will add storage, and you can also place the dishwasher and sink in there, so they are out of the way. There is no house that has enough storage, so adding this will be a huge plus. If you are able to add storage in other ways in the kitchen, you can look at doing that as well.

Create a Modern Bathroom

Like mentioned above, the bathroom is something that people

are looking for in a property. It can actually make or break a sale or booking. When people are looking at a vacation rental, one of the things they are most curious about is the bathroom. A bathroom is where someone should feel most comfortable and relaxed. Upgrading the space to feature a more modern design is going to go a long way.

One feature that seems to be a huge drawcard is a double sink vanity. This adds more counter space as well as more storage under the sink. It also makes the bathroom feel more modern and spacious. More than one person can get ready in the morning, and this will allow bathroom time to be more efficient. This is especially necessary in an ensuite bathroom in the main bedroom. Along with this, you should look into making the bathroom feel very light and open. Older bathrooms were often filled with darker colors as well as browns. This makes the space look very dated and unclean. You can't go wrong with white in a bathroom.

Improve the Outdoor Space

There are many outdoor features that can increase the value of a property. These things will also make it a more attractive space for short-term renters. People love spending time outdoors, and making the space functional and aesthetic will go a long way. If you have a house, you will have a lot more space to use and upgrade. Apartments are a different story. You can still implement some of the tips if you have a balcony or a small ground floor garden.

A pool can add huge value to a house. This is good for those looking to sell the house or who are using it as a vacation rental. If you are looking to sell the house, you will have to market it to someone who does want a pool. There are some people who could not be bothered to look after the pool, but most homebuyers would love them. If you are renting out the home, pool care is something you will need to budget for. If a pool is not feasible, you could try a hot tub. This gives a very high-end feel, and most people really enjoy it. You could get one built into the ground or a freestanding one, depending on the space available.

An outdoor deck is also a great investment. Having a place for friends and family to gather outdoors is something most people are looking for. Trendy outdoor spaces are very much needed. You could also include an outdoor cooking space, which will further increase the value. A fireplace or fire pit is another addition to the deck or general outdoor space that can add value. An outdoor space should be a place for people to gather and enjoy themselves. Anything you add that will have this effect will add value to the home.

Build an ADU

ADU stands for accessory dwelling unit. This is a space that is separate from the main house that someone else can stay in. This is also known as a granny cottage or in-law suite. It will be fully equipped with its own kitchen, bathroom, and living space but will be much smaller than the main home. You will need space on the property to build this, so it might not be feasible for everyone.

This type of renovation has benefits for many types of investors. If you are looking to sell the property, its value will increase. People with bigger families would be drawn to a place like this as it has more space and is a convenient living solution for someone who doesn't want to live with the rest of the family all the time and seeks some privacy. Many families stay with many generations of their families, and this is growing in popularity. Even if the family does not want to use it like this, there are many other uses. Perhaps it can be converted to a home office away from the main house. Another option is that the owners could rent out this space to make additional income. If you are not looking to sell the home, there are still benefits. You will be able to rent out the space separately and make more rental income. As long as there is a separate entrance and privacy from the main home, this can make an additional income. Students, singles, and new couples would not mind staying in a space like this because it will be affordable. This means you are able to make two rental incomes from one property. You can use the same strategy if you are renting out short-term. These are two separate spaces that can be rented out for different purposes. Singles, couples, and those on a budget would be able to rent out the smaller space, and those who are on a budget have the option of the smaller space, while those on the opposite side of the spectrum have the larger one.

> If you are not looking to sell the home, there are still benefits. You will be able to rent out the space separately and make more rental income. As long as there is a separate entrance and privacy from the main home, this can make an additional income.

Inspections

Inspections are an important part of owning a property. This is especially true when you are renting it out. You want to make sure that everything is running smoothly and that if there are any problems, you sort them out sooner rather than later. You can run inspections whenever you want, as long as you are not intrusive to those living on your property. As much as inspections are important, you do have to be mindful that other people are using the space. If this is a long-term rental, this is especially important to the people for whom your renters are using this as their home. You don't want to be a landlord who chases away their tenants. If you notify tenants in advance, then there shouldn't be too much of a problem.

Move-In Inspection

An inspection should be done before the tenant moves in or guest comes to stay. This is crucial, so you know that everything is as it should be. For a long-term rental, you need to check that all safety regulations have been met and that the property is in the best condition it can be. It is a good idea to take photos of the space to ensure that you know how you left it. The move-in inspection is not only to provide the tenant with what they need but also for you to check up on the property.

If the tenant causes any damage to the property, you don't want them to claim that it was like that when they got there. This will make it difficult to claim from insurance or to get them to pay for it. If you have a phone or camera, you can take a video of the home before the tenant moves in. Make sure you take note of any damage that is already there. Video the walls, ceilings, plumbing, electrical sockets, fixtures, cupboards, doors, and any furniture you have on the property. If the video is not timestamped, you can send the video to yourself using email, so you have proof of when it was taken.

If you are running a short-term rental, you should be doing an inspection before every check in. This is not necessarily a full inspection, but to make sure that everything is in order and in the right place. You will need to replace anything that has been used up or broken since your last stay. It is important to stay consistent when it comes to running a rental because you might have repeat guests. They will be expecting the same level of care and quality.

Move-Out Inspection

The move-out inspection will be done after the current tenants have moved out. You can actually do this inspection before they hand over the keys. You will need to use the videos and photos you took upon their moving in. This is to make sure that everything is in the same condition. General wear and tear shouldn't be too much of an issue but take note of any big problems. You will also have to do a general inspection to make sure the home is ready for the next tenants to move in. It is best to do this as the current tenants are moving out, so you have some time to fix things that need to be attended to. Everything that we discussed in the section concerning preventive property maintenance will apply here too.

If you are running a short-term rental, you will need to do an inspection after each guest checks out. You should aim to do this as soon as possible after they check out because, if there are any issues, you can take them up with them immediately. You will also need to give them back their security deposit if you have taken one, so doing the inspection before then is essential. If there are damages that have occurred, you can either keep the security deposit or go through the process of asking them for payment for bigger damages. You will also need to log it with your insurance so you can get paid out as soon as possible. You should also do a general inspection to make sure the property is ready for the next guests. Check all the plumbing, fixtures, electronics, and appliances to make sure they are still working. You will also have to reset and restage the property. Taking pictures of the setup can help you recreate it exactly the same each time.

Seasonal Inspection

A seasonal inspection helps you keep the property well maintained. This is not to check up on the tenants but to make sure the property is ready for changes in season. If you live in a country or state that has drastic weather changes each season, then these will be needed. Countries and states that have mild seasonal changes might not have to worry about this too much, but certain aspects still apply.

In the winter, you will need to make sure the heating is working properly and that the appliances are in good condition. If the renters have their own appliances, then you don't need to worry about that. You will need to check for any water leaks, as this could lead to freezing in the colder months. Since the stove will be used a lot more during this time, you want to check the hood for any buildup and change the filter if necessary. The water heater should be checked for leaks and pressure problems since this will be needed during the cold months.

After winter, there could be some damage to your property. This is why a spring inspection is needed. Check the exterior of the property to make sure that there is no damage, cracks, or leaks. You should also have a look at the roof, as these tend to get hit the hardest if you have had winter storms. Check the driveways and pavements for cracks and damage. This can cause trips and injuries, so it is best to get them fixed as soon as you can. All water sources should be checked. This includes the ones outdoors because these might not have been used during the winter and will need to be researched for the spring.

A summer inspection will include making sure all the fun stuff on the property is working well. Check the wooden deck for damage and look into resealing it, as this will extend its life. Your plants and lawn will need to be taken care of and inspected. General water leaks and damage checks will also need to be done.

The fall is the time for things to start winding down again. You will need to start protecting your outdoor water sources. Covering them up to prevent them from freezing and cracking is important. Ensure that the gutters have been cleaned towards the end of fall so that there isn't any build up from the falling leaves. You might have to drain your pool if your property is in a colder climate, as you do not want it to freeze. Make sure all the heating equipment is working well and has been maintained.

Chapter 10

Your Real Estate Portfolio

Real Estate provides the highest returns, the greatest values, and the least risk.

–Armstrong Williams

When you are a real estate investor, there are plenty of options on how you can go about it. As you continue investing and get more experienced, you might want to grow your portfolio. It is a really good idea to work toward a diversified portfolio so that you can protect yourself financially. They say that we shouldn't put all our eggs in one basket, and that rings true when it comes to investing. If you only have one type of investment, if something were to happen to the market, it would be a huge loss for you. However, if you have various different investments, you don't have to stress out too much if something goes wrong in one area. You have enough capital in the other investments to hold you until the other market picks back up again.

Single-Family Business Investing

Single-family home investing is something that is becoming more popular. People are looking for larger properties for their families to live in, and multigenerational living is on the rise. This means that people will be looking for a place for themselves and their families. This is definitely a niche that you can get into, and it is much easier to manage each property since you only have to worry about one point of contact. This is also more of a long-term commitment, which means you could have a stable income from the property for a long time to come. When you rent out a single-family home, it is not uncommon for them to stay in the home for multiple years. All you have to do is make sure the general matters are taken care of.

With this kind of investment, you might have to give over more control to the tenant. Since it is their home, they might want to make some improvements so it feels like a home to them. Renovations might still be off the table, but make sure you stipulate what is and isn't allowed. Renovations might not be a bad idea if they are willing to pay for them. You just need to clear the designs first and make sure you are still in control of the investment.

When you are looking to invest in this type of property, you need to choose the right location. Not every location will attract the type of family looking to stay for a long time. If you buy a property in the city, it will likely be smaller. and there is a higher likelihood of people moving in and out. This is not necessarily a bad thing, but it is not what you want with this type of strategy. Think about what a family would be looking for in a property. A place close to schools, shopping centers, transportation, and other amenities would be ideal. A property in a safe neighborhood is also ideal. The neighborhood will determine the type of person you attract, so make sure you do your research in this regard.

Multifamily Investing

A multifamily property is one that will house multiple families on one property. This doesn't mean that each family will be living with another. It is two separate units with their own kitchens and bathrooms, but on one property. If you own an apartment block or duplex. This would count as a multifamily home. Each family will live in close proximity to the other. The term "daily" does not have to be in the traditional sense of a couple and children. This could be a single person or even a group of friends living together. In this context, the term is just used to refer to a group of people.

This type of investing can be costly at first. If you think about it, you are purchasing multiple homes. It does take a substantial amount of money to do that. You will need to have your finances in order before you can invest like this. You will be able to get a loan, but you must still have enough spare money for the down payment. This does take some planning so don't feel discouraged if you can't make this kind of investment within a short timeframe. With this being said, it might be easier for you to secure financing for a multifamily home. This is because the cash flow of this kind of investment is more predictable and stable than that of a single-family home.

Let's say you own a complex with five units. If someone were to move out without warning, you would end up losing around 20% of your overall income, but you would still be able to pay your mortgage because the other four units are still making money. You have some time to look for a new tenant without it becoming a huge problem. If the same thing happens to a single-family home, all income would be lost, and this is risky for a bank or mortgage provider. The bank will have more confidence and therefore offer lower interest rates, but you will need to shop around to find the best rates.

The other benefit is that you can have one loan that covers all the units. This means you can make multiple incomes from the one loan. With single-family investing, you will need to take out a new loan for each property, and this can be difficult to manage. You have a good chance of turning multifamily homes into a passive income stream because you can hire a property manager to take care of everything for you. You will only have to worry about the big things, and the tenants won't even contact you for anything. Since you will be making a larger sum of money, it will be easier to pay for a property manager. Even though you can charge more for a single-family home, the quantity of properties involved will end up making you more money.

Commercial Real Estate Investing

Commercial real estate can be a great way to diversify your current investments. It is a completely different market from family home investing because a different demographic of people are looking for these kinds of properties. There are also various types of commercial real estate that you could invest in. Retail spaces, office buildings, and warehouses are just some of the commercial real estate you can invest in. Commercial just means that it is used for business and to take part in activities that will bring in money. People need these spaces for a whole host of reasons, and this means your portfolio can be diversified even more based on the sectors your real estate caters to.

Since people who rent out your space have their own businesses, they are going to be more professional. They need the space in order to make money, so they will do their best to maintain a formal and positive relationship with you or your property manager. This means that you can rely on them paying their rent more regularly. They have their reputation on the line as well. This is not to say that all business owners will act professionally. There are all types of people in the world, and some can act out of character. You should always be prepared for a few encounters when you have a property business. It comes with the territory.

Your property will be in the public eye. People who use property for businesses will need to maintain it well. Since meetings take place on the property or there are customers coming in and out, appearance really matters. This means there is some security in terms of how your investment will be handled. Again, this is not a rule because you can always get a tenant that does not care for their space as well as you would like. However, in general, people who run businesses will take care of their space as best they can, so they do not harm their own reputation.

Even though it is the tenants' responsibility to keep the property well looked after, there does come some risk. Commercial properties have more people in and out of them than residential properties. You never know who these people are and some of them could cause some damages to the property out of no fault of the renter. There is also general wear and tear to take into consideration. Since the traffic in and out of the property is going to be higher, you will have to expect more maintenance issues. This does come at a cost and will require a larger time commitment if you are doing most things yourself. There is also the risk of vandals and crimes taking place in commercial properties. Even though these things can take place on any property, commercial property is at a higher risk. However, it does depend on the area the property is in and the type of business running from it.

One benefit that most people don't think about is the fact that commercial properties typically close after work hours. This can be a good thing if you are running the property yourself. You will likely not get any calls at odd hours of the night about something property related. Most of these things will be handled during regular hours. As a landlord, you will have to take care of the property to some extent. If there is an issue, then you will need to meet your tenants' needs. When it comes to family homes, there is no time frame. In fact, there is a higher chance of something going wrong outside of work hours because people are at home during those times. This can be quite inconvenient. When it comes to commercial properties, unless there is a real emergency, you can be sure that you will only be called up at appropriate hours of the day.

Commercial properties could also be more secure in terms of your rental income. This is highly dependent on the type of business that is running, but most businesses look to plant in a location for a long time. Moving around could cause their customers and clients to get confused, which could cause other issues. If the businesses that run out of your properties are serious and well established then you can be sure that they will stick around for a long time, possibly even permanently. This does add a layer of security to your income. With this being said, it might take some time to find these kinds of residents. Vetting your tenants is really important, especially if you want to create a certain type of culture within the building. Some people or businesses might not be the best choices, so it is okay to deny someone a lease for a specific reason. This will be a learning curve, just like most things when it comes to real estate investing.

The great thing about real estate investing is that you are able to diversify within the niche. You can do so much based on what you need and want. As you gain more experience, you might decide to take on more advanced forms of real estate investing. If you are managing your properties well, banks and financial institutions will be more likely to give you bigger loans. This means you can start investing more and increase your overall profits. You also have the opportunity to turn some of your properties into passive income through the services of a property management company. This will result in more free time for you to do whatever you would like. As you grow with your investments, you are able to free up more options and flexibility for yourself.

Chapter 11

Tax Benefits

Landlords grow rich in their sleep.

–John Stuart Mill

Nobody likes the taxman. In fact, almost all of us are on the lookout for ways we can lower the amount of money we pay in taxes. At the end of the day, we want to keep as much of the money we earn for ourselves. There is nothing wrong with that. Real estate is one of the best ways we can cut down on taxes legally, so we don't have to give away our hard earned cash. Let me just say that paying your taxes is important. It is a fact of life that we live under a government. Things need to get done in society, and that is why we pay taxes. However, there is no need to pay more than is necessary, and if there are ways around paying exorbitant taxes, then why not do them.

Real Estate Tax Benefits

There are many different ways you can use real estate to reduce your taxes. This can often be confusing for most people, which is why getting an accountant or tax practitioner is usually the best way to go. Yes, it does come at an additional cost, but it will be worth it because you know everything is taken care of and you are not missing anything. You should also take into consideration the time it takes to do your own taxes and the fact that most people miss out on tax breaks. The tax law is also changing all the time. Staying on top of things can be a hassle. If you are capable, you should definitely do it, but there is no shame in getting a bit of help while you focus on other things.

> You should also take into consideration the time it takes to do your own taxes and the fact that most people miss out on tax breaks.

Depreciation

Depreciation is when an investment starts to lose value. A property can depreciate over time due to the general wear and tear that occurs. This has nothing to do with the actual cash flow of your property. You could still be making a large profit and qualify for depreciation when it comes to taxes. Depreciation will also be counted as a net loss for your property, regardless of how much you make from it. In order for this to work, a system called "modified accelerated cost recovery" is used. The overall amount you will be paying for taxes will come down if you qualify for this.

1031 Exchange

You can cut down on taxes if you exchange one property for another. This might sound like a strange deal, but it does work. You will need to make the exchange between two properties that are very similar. In most cases, an asset swap will result in you being taxed when the sale takes place. This is not the case here. There are actually quite a few scenarios where you can take advantage of this. Let's say you already own a property, and another one goes on the market. The new property is very similar to the one you currently have, but it is in a better location, so you will end up making a lot more money from it. You can use this method to buy the other property and forego much of your taxes. You can also purchase a new property that is higher in value than the one you currently have. The 1031 exchange is basically just using the equity from one property to purchase another one.

There are rules in place that need to be followed in order to qualify for this. For example, you will not be able to use the equity to purchase a property of lesser value. You will also need to purchase a property of the same kind. This means if you have a residential property, you will not be able to purchase another kind of real estate, such as a commercial property or a REIT. The properties in question both have to be used for investing purposes and nothing else. If you meet all of these criteria, then you will likely get approval and can move forward.

You should also be aware of the time limit that is set for the transactions. You do not have all the time in the world, as the time frame is quite short. You only have 45 days to send a list of the properties you are willing to purchase after the sale of your current property. There is also a limit to the number of properties you can put forward, so be aware of that. You will also have to purchase the new property within 180 days of selling the old one (Artzberger, 2021). These rules need to be followed in order for you to qualify, so you do have to make sure everything is lined up.

Tax Deductions

When you own a property, there are certain expenses that will count as tax deductions. This means the amount of money that counts as taxable will be reduced. You will be taxed on the money after all of the expenses are taken care of. This will help you pay far less in taxes. Understanding what tax deductible is, is really important for you to save money. The types of deductions you can get will depend on your state or country and can change at any time. This is why it is important to do your research and make sure you are in the know about what is going on in the world of taxes.

There is a difference between the tax implications of a residential property and an investment property. An investment property is one that generates income for you. This means it is almost treated like a business. When you have a business, there are certain tax benefits placed upon you, and this is why real estate investing comes with tax perks. You will be able to deduct expenses that come from the running, managing, and operating of the property. You can talk to an accountant to find out the full extent of this, but we will be going through a few of them in this section.

Insurance

We have already spoken about the importance of insurance. You should make sure your property is covered for certain things, so you do not have to get into debt or pay out huge lump sums when something unexpected happens. Insurance can also have tax benefits when you have an investment property. This is yet another reason to get some insurance.

You shouldn't get a whole bunch of unnecessary insurance policies, but make sure you are covered for all the important things. You will have to prove that you are paying insurance before this is taken as a tax write-off. This is a motivating factor to get some insurance if you were on the fence about it.

Property Taxes

A property tax is put on you when you purchase a property in a certain area. This is run by the local governments. These taxes are used to pay for and maintain the amenities in the area. Certain areas will have a higher property tax than others because of what is made available to the residents. It is important to do your research on the area before you buy a property. You don't want to be hit with a huge tax bill out of nowhere.

When you are researching the area, you should find out what you are getting for the taxes you are paying. The amount should be worth it. A good area will always be a huge draw and benefit you as an investor. This means your area of choice might come with higher taxes than other areas. In many cases, you will receive one large bill that covers multiple things, so you don't have to pay your taxes separately from things like utilities.

When you are just a regular resident, you will be expected to pay your property taxes and move on. However, a real estate investor can count this as a business expense and get a tax right off for all or a portion of the property tax. This will bring down the overall amount being paid and could also mean you can afford to purchase a property that has a higher amount of tax owed.

Property Management Fees

A property management company can help you turn your investments into passive income. You can leave everything up to them, and they will handle your property like a dream. If your tenants have any queries or concerns, they will be directed to the property manager, so you do not have to get involved. The level of service you get will depend on your needs as well as what the property management company offers. Property management does not qualify as a business expense, so you will be able to lower your net income if you do use a company to help manage your property.

Advertising Expenses

There is a lot that goes into running a business, and a real estate investing business is no exception. You will need to put some money into advertising as your business grows, but the good news is that it can be a tax-deductible expense.

Software, Tools, or Other Real Estate Support Expenses

If you use any tools or software to run your real estate investment business, this can be a write off as well. You just have to show that you are using it for your business. There are many support expenses that can be counted. You just need to prove that you are using it for your business. Even if you use part of the tools or software for your own personal use, it can still be labeled as a business expense if you are predominantly using it for this reason.

Legal Fees

Any legal fees that are incurred through running your real estate investment business could be a write off. Again, it all comes down to proving you used it for business. You will be using a lawyer for many different things when you are in this business. The fees can be expensive but at least there is this benefit.

Closing Costs Such as Title Company and Lender Fees

Closing costs come on top of the amount you and the seller have decided on. Since this is a business expense, you will be able to write it off on your taxes. Remember to have all your paperwork in order when it comes to this. You will not be able to have taxes deducted if you cannot produce the relevant proof and paperwork.

Home Office Expenses

You will likely have some home office expenses when running your real estate investment business. Things like Wi-Fi, stationery, and office equipment like printers, could all count as business expenses. You might even be able to have a portion of your home loan or mortgage be tax deductible. Many people who work from home will have their home office be tax deductible because they use it for work purposes. You will need to measure the size of your home office and find the percentage against the total area of your home. This is the percentage that will be tax deductible. Even though you might use this space for other things or because it is part of your house, it doesn't really matter. You might be able to use it to pay a smaller amount of tax.

It is a good idea to make a list of everything you use for your business. If you go out to purchase stationery or anything else that might be used to help with your real estate investment business, keep the proof. If you buy a new laptop or another piece of technology, this could also help lower your taxes. You will have to be strategic about this, but if you do it right, you will be able to lower your taxable income by a good amount.

Travel and Mileage Expenses

If you need to travel for your real estate investment business, then you can deduct the expenses as well. This applies regardless of how you travel. You can deduct travel expenses such as plane, bus, or train tickets; Uber rides; taxis; hotel stays; and gas or other vehicle expenses. It all depends on the mode of transportation you are using for your business. You will also need to prove that you are traveling for business. If your property is in another city or state, then it might be necessary for you to fly there, and therefore the plane tickets, hotel stay, and other traveling expenses could be tax deductible.

There are plenty of tax benefits that come into play when you are investing in real estate. Some people deem this unfair, but the truth is that these are incentives. It is good when people engage in business activities. Not only does it help them grow their own finances, but it is good for the economy as a whole. A healthy and growing economy is essential for any country. You are contributing to yourself and to the country you live in when you engage in business activities. That is something to be proud of. Not everyone wants to be a property investor, and not everyone can be one. If you are someone who can, then you should be able to benefit from the tax breaks you get.

Chat to your accountant and see what advice they give you. When you have real estate or any other kind of business, a good accountant is essential. There are a lot of moving parts when it comes to your finances, and having someone there to advise you and help you make the right financial decisions is crucial. It's one less thing to worry about. You can take your time finding the right person because building a good relationship is ideal. You are trusting that person with your money which is no small thing. Make sure the person is right for you and you will never regret it.

Conclusion

When one door closes, buy another one and open it yourself.

–Anonymous

The quote above is truly a beautiful one. Even though we do not know who said it, we can see this person is one who takes matters into their own hands. When you are on a real estate investment journey, it is all about taking the bull by the horns and diving in. There are so many people who want to become real estate investors but for some reason or another they end up putting it off. There will always be excuses not to do something. It is human nature to not venture off into the unknown, but the problem is that we end up stunting our own growth. It is essential for us to keep trying and keep opening new doors for ourselves.

This real estate investment journey is not going to be a cake walk. If you look at all the famous investors, they will be able to tell you about all the hard times and the sacrifices they made to get to where they are now. They will also tell you how they would do everything again. It is within the journey that we learn so much. We end up growing and becoming better people for it. You will be learning throughout the process, and you will learn to become a better investor.

Many people believe they can read a book or take a course and that will make them great investors. These tools can help, and I certainly hope this book helps you, but these are just tools. You have to pick them up and use them. This book is simply a blueprint, but you have to do something with what you have learned. You will need to take the time to develop a plan and make it work for yourself. Granted, you are in a much better starting position than many because you have the right base knowledge. This means you can avoid some of the common mistakes and get a head start. This puts you on the right path for success, but it is up to you to take the steps to get there.

> Many people believe they can read a book or take a course and that will make them great investors. These tools can help, and I certainly hope this book helps you, but these are just tools. You have to pick them up and use them.

The information in this book might seem like a lot, but you can make it a bit more manageable. Rather than looking at it as one huge book, break it down. You have a good overview of what is in the book, and you can go back to the relevant chapters as you are at different points in your journey. This will help you practically as you move through the different stages of becoming a real estate investor.

If you are looking for a place to start, why not get some inspiration? Start looking at properties and think about the type of investments you want to make. You can start looking at the prices as well as the features you like. This will help you get an idea of the market and will inspire you in the present. Once you understand how much you will need, you can start saving for a down payment on a property. If you do not have a lot of money to start with, it is time to make a budget. Even if the goal seems far away, you have to start somewhere. Make a strategy for saving and growing your down payment savings. This is taking steps in the right direction. Eventually you will have enough, and you can start investing. Once you get to this stage, things happen quickly, so you can mentally prepare yourself until you get there.

I firmly believe that investing in real estate is one of the best things a person can do for themselves. It helps you be reliant on yourself and have the security you need in your life. You are allowing yourself the opportunity to build wealth and build the life you want. This is to be commended. I wish you luck on your journey and hope you continue taking steps forward and gaining knowledge that will lead you to success.

References

Artzberger, W. (2021, December 9). *How to use real estate to put off tax bills.* Investopedia. https://www.investopedia.com/articles/tax/08/real-estate-reduce-tax.asp

Beattie, A. (2022, July 14). *4 simple ways to invest in real estate.* Investopedia. https://www.investopedia.com/investing/simple-ways-invest-real-estate/

Braun, K. (2021, September 17). *Real estate investing for beginners: Getting started.* Clever Girl Finance. https://www.clevergirlfinance.com/blog/real-estate-investing-for-beginners/

Bungalow. (2022, February 1). *Best room and home rentals experience.* Bungalow. https://bungalow.com/articles/what-to-consider-before-multifamily-investing

Byrne, S. (2021, May 24). *Council post: Exploring the tax benefits of real estate investing.* Forbes. https://www.forbes.com/sites/forbesbusinesscouncil/2021

/05/24/exploring-the-tax-benefits-of-real-estate-investing/?sh=3bfd80b53fff

Chen, J. (2022, July 20). *Commercial real estate gives businesses homes.* Investopedia. https://www.investopedia.com/terms/c/commercialrealestate.asp

Collins, A. (2022, June 20). *How to create a referral marketing strategy [+definition].* Shopify. https://www.shopify.com/uk/blog/15679636-referral-marketing-101-7-tactics-to-launch-your-own-referral-campaign

Cote, C. (2021, August 24). *How to analyze a real estate investment.* HBS Online. https://online.hbs.edu/blog/post/real-estate-investment-analysis

Covrigaru, K. (2022, May 3). *Council post: Five tips for successful single-family rental investing.* Forbes. https://www.forbes.com/sites/forbesbusinesscouncil/2022/05/03/five-tips-for-successful-single-family-rental-investing/?sh=14ea9e6b6fa8

Creating an investment plan. (n.d.). Collective Shift. https://collectiveshift.io/topic/creating-an-investment-plan/#:~:text=When%20developing%20an%20investment%20plan%2C%20you%20should%20start

Daibes, V. (2017, July 29). *7 major benefits of investing in real estate.* Investment Property Tips | Mashvisor Real Estate Blog. https://www.mashvisor.com/blog/benefits-of-investing-in-real-estate/#:~:text=The%20Benefits%20of%20Real%20Estate%20Investing%201%201.

Deming, M. (2019, January 31). *The landlord's preventative property maintenance checklist.* Avail. https://www.avail.co/education/guides/complete-guide-to-rental-property-maintenance/preventative-maintenance-checklist

Direct and indirect real estate investment. (2021, January 8). Kacie Business. https://kaciebusiness.com/what-is-real-estate-investment-direct-and-indirect-real-estate-investment/

Epperhart, B. (2021, September 27). *8 benefits of real estate investing.* Wealth Builders. https://www.wealthbuilders.org/benefits-of-real-estate-investing/

Esajian, P. (2022, August 31). *Here's why you should be raw land investing.* FortuneBuilders. https://www.fortunebuilders.com/how-to-know-if-raw-land-investing-is-right-for-you/

Folger, J. (2021, August 30). *Direct real estate investing versus REITs.* Investopedia. https://www.investopedia.com/articles/investing/072314/investing-real-estate-versus-reits.asp

Fontinelle, A. (2022, September 12). *9 things to know about homeowners associations.* Investopedia.

https://www.investopedia.com/articles/mortgages-real-estate/08/homeowners-associations-tips.asp

Hare, D. (2021, May 6). *How to invest in raw land and make money in 2022.* APXN Property. https://apxnproperty.com/raw-land-investing/

Herrig, A. (2019, July 2). *Is investing in real estate worth it? (6 lessons from an actual investor).* Wealthy Nickel. https://wealthynickel.com/is-investing-in-real-estate-worth-it/

How to conduct a property analysis before purchasing a rental property. (n.d.). UniversalClass. https://www.universalclass.com/articles/business/property-buying-as-a-property-manager.htm

Jahnke, T. (2019, June 18). *11 must-know facts about residential real estate investing.* Learn.roofstock.com. https://learn.roofstock.com/blog/residential-real-estate-investing

Kalfrin, V. (2022, February 4). *How to tell which renovations increase your home's value.* HomeLight Blog. https://www.homelight.com/blog/which-renovations-increase-home-value/

Kline, B. (2020, June 3). *The most important statistics for real estate investing.* Realtybiznews. https://realtybiznews.com/the-most-important-statistics-for-real-estate-investing-2/98758942/

Larson, M. (2013, July 30). *Pros and cons of investing in commercial real estate.* Nolo. https://www.nolo.com/legal-encyclopedia/pros-cons-investing-commercial-real-estate.html

Linden, D. (2019, October 22). *House hunting? Here are 5 different types of real estate loans.* Daisy Linden. https://daisylinden.com/types-of-real-estate-loans/#:~:text=Here%20are%205%20different%20types%20of%20real%20estate

MailChimp. (n.d.). *What is email marketing? Definition and advantages.* Mailchimp. https://mailchimp.com/en-gb/marketing-glossary/email-marketing/

Mayer, L. (2022, February 23). *Why is liquidity important in the real estate industry?* Linkedin. https://www.linkedin.com/pulse/why-liquidity-important-real-estate-industry-leon-mayer?trk=public_profile_article_view

McCormick, K. (2022, November 10). *27 free & low-budget marketing ideas for any business.* Wordstream. https://www.wordstream.com/blog/ws/2020/12/09/free-and-low-budget-marketing-ideas

McCracken, M. (2022, March 18). *Real estate 101: How to analyze investment properties.* Bay Property Management Group. https://www.baymgmtgroup.com/blog/analyze-investment-properties/

Powderly, D. (2016, March 7). *The differences between direct and indirect real estate investing.* Linkedin. https://www.linkedin.com/pulse/differences-between-direct-indirect-real-estate-darren-powderly

Property tax: What it is & how to calculate. (n.d.). Www.rocketmortgage.com. https://www.rocketmortgage.com/learn/property-tax

Real estate crowdfunding. (2022, August 31). Investopedia. https://www.investopedia.com/ask/answers/100214/what-real-estate-crowdfunding.asp#:~:text=Real%20estate%20crowdfunding%20uses%20social%20media%20and%20the

Real estate market analysis: What it is & how to do it. (2021, October 11). QuestionPro. https://www.questionpro.com/blog/real-estate-market-analysis/#:~:text=What%20is%20a%20real%20estate

Real estate investing guide. (2022, June 28). Investopedia. https://www.investopedia.com/mortgage/real-estate-investing-guide/

Seasonal home maintenance checklist. (n.d.). The BrickKicker. https://www.brickkicker.com/seasonal-home-maintenance-checklist/

Sutika, M. (2022, May 25). *10 types of insurance for real estate investors to consider.* Obierisk. https://www.obierisk.com/blog/insurance-for-real-estate-investors

Top 6 tax benefits of real estate investing. (n.d.). Www.rocketmortgage.com. https://www.rocketmortgage.com/learn/tax-benefits-of-real-estate-investing

Wall, K. (2021, October 21). *The best low-cost marketing tactics for your business - A quick guide | markletic.* Www.markletic.com. https://www.markletic.com/blog/the-best-low-cost-marketing-tactics-for-your-business-a-quick-guide/

Weiss, R. J. (2021, October 13). *How to start investing for beginners [step by step].* The Ways to Wealth. https://www.thewaystowealth.com/investing/how-to-start-investing/

West, M. (2018). *10 inspirational quotes for your real estate business.* Animoto. https://animoto.com/blog/business/inspirational-quotes-real-estate-business

What is A portfolio loan? (n.d.). Neal Business Funding. https://nealfunding.com/what-is-a-portfolio-loan/#:~:text=Portfolio%20loans%20are%20often%20utilized%20by%20investors%20who

Wichter, Z. (2022, January 10). *This seasonal home maintenance checklist will keep your house in shape.* Bankrate. https://www.bankrate.com/real-estate/seasonal-home-maintenance-checklist/

Willens, J. (2022). *30 inspiring real estate quotes that will change your life*. Realwealth. https://realwealth.com/learn/real-estate-quotes/

www.ingramcontent.com/pod-product-compliance
Lightning Source LLC
Chambersburg PA
CBHW031421210526
45464CB00005B/1986